Utilizing Teacher Aides
in the Classroom

Utilizing Teacher Aides in the Classroom

By

DICK B. CLOUGH, Ed.D.

Principal
Strong Elementary School
Marianna, Arkansas

and

BONNIE M. CLOUGH, M.Ed.

Third Grade Teacher
Strong Elementary School
Marianna, Arkansas

CHARLES C THOMAS • PUBLISHER
Springfield • Illinois • U.S.A.

Published and Distributed Throughout the World by
CHARLES C THOMAS • PUBLISHER
Bannerstone House
301-327 East Lawrence Avenue, Springfield, Illinois, U.S.A.

© *1978, by* CHARLES C THOMAS • PUBLISHER
ISBN 0-398-03741-8
Library of Congress Catalog Card Number: 77-15410

With THOMAS BOOKS *careful attention is given to all details of
manufacturing and design. It is the Publisher's desire to present books that
are satisfactory as to their physical qualities and artistic possibilities and
appropriate for their particular use.* THOMAS BOOKS *will be true to those
laws of quality that assure a good name and good will.*

Printed in the United States of America
R-11

Library of Congress Cataloging in Publication Data

Clough, Dick B
    Utilizing teacher aides in the classroom.

    Bibliography: p.
    Includes index.
    1. Teachers' assistants. I. Clough, Bonnie M.,
joint author. II. Title.
LB2844.1.A8C56   371.1'412   77-15410
ISBN 0-398-03741-8

INTRODUCTION

ONE has to spend only a few minutes in an elementary classroom to realize that the teacher must be kind of a jack-of-all-trades — bookkeeper, nurse, clerk, handyman, and maid. In between, she must try to teach more subject matter in what seems to her to be less time than ever before. These increased demands upon today's teacher have led most school boards throughout the nation to provide funds to employ non-certified persons to assist classroom teachers in a variety of ways. Teacher aide programs are now an established part of the school program in more and more school districts across the nation.

However, if classroom aides are to be effective instructional assistants, teachers must develop some expertise in utilizing their talents. Many elementary teachers look upon their aides as nothing more than clerical assistants and provide the aides with little opportunity to become involved in instructional activities. Generally speaking, aides have been limited to clerical or housekeeping duties such as correcting papers, operating audiovisual equipment, preparing bulletin boards, and keeping records. While all of these tasks are necessary and useful, most teachers fail to recognize the advantages of utilizing classroom aides in working with children in the teaching-learning process. Too often, these supportive personnel have little contact with children in cognitive and affective areas of the curriculum.

Who is to blame for this failure to accept and use classroom aides for direct instructional and emotional support to children? Perhaps educators have overemphasized the importance of having four years of college-level training prior to entry into the teaching ranks. Maybe this reluctance on the part of teachers is a result of a desire to protect their professional standing. Or, more likely, it is a result of the inability of elementary teachers to "know how" to effectively utilize the talents and abilities of individual aides.

Utilizing Teacher Aides in the Classroom has been designed to help classroom teachers develop managerial and human relations skills essential in working with noncertificated personnel. Its content is based upon the premise that, with preparation and training, teacher aides can contribute to the effectiveness of the classroom environment far beyond the limits usually set for them. This contribution will initially permit more time for the teacher to assess student needs and evaluate programs, while ultimately improving the quality of classroom instruction. Additionally, utilization of classroom aides will help children benefit from the special talents and friendship of the aide.

CONTENTS

Utilizing Teacher Aides
in the Classroom

CHAPTER 1

THE TEACHER AND THE AIDE

MOST of the recent literature on teacher aides has dwelt on the aides' duties and responsibilities, with little attention being directed toward the classroom teacher's role in utilizing aides. Yet many teachers confess to varying degrees of ignorance when it comes to knowing how to effectively utilize the talents and abilities of classroom aides. More often than not, aides have not been trained to assist teachers, and likewise, teachers have not been trained to use aides. It is rare indeed to find a teacher training program that adequately prepares teachers to work with another adult in their classrooms.

Those who have worked with several aides soon realize that just as teachers come in all different sizes, shapes, and competencies, so do classroom aides. If you are fortunate enough to be assigned an aide who is truly talented in every respect upon the day of her arrival, you can be confident the task ahead will be a thoroughly enjoyable one. The truth of the matter, however, is that few aides appear with such all-impressive credentials. Indeed, in most instances, the classroom teacher must provide the aide's growth experiences.

In addition, many teachers fail to realize that a successful aide program depends in large measure upon a thorough understanding of the purposes and goals of the program. Misunderstandings will be avoided if roles and functions of both teachers and aides are clearly understood. Teachers working with aides must rely upon their own judgment in assigning duties to their aide. A tactful, perceptive teacher should help the aide to realize that her duty is to assist the teacher and not to take liberties or assume authority for which she is not professionally trained.

There is a whole range of activities a teacher aide can perform, depending on her skills and educational background.

Some who have had at least three years of college and are at the level of student teachers can handle many instructional duties. Even though most aides are only high school graduates, they can do a great deal to assist the teacher in caring for children. They can provide the person-to-person contact so many children need, they can give a child warmth and comfort when a teacher is not able to, and they can listen to a child with a problem.

However, the exact nature of the kind of tasks the aide will perform in the classroom will largely depend upon the aide's and your own capabilities and the rapport and understanding you are able to develop with each other. The assistance an instructional aide can provide is really limited only by your and the aide's imagination. Likewise, while suggestions can be given classroom teachers, no one plan for utilization of an aide's time will work in every situation.

BASIC OBJECTIVES

The teacher aide is employed so that the professional teacher may direct her energies toward the child's education. The implementation of an aide program may cause an adjustment in the teacher's duties. However, teachers will not spend less time in teaching. They will spend more time planning and implementing instructional techniques, guiding and counseling pupils, and carrying out other instructional activities that will upgrade the professional attention given the student.

The basic objectives for the use of teacher aides are as follows:

1. To make it possible for teachers to use more variety in structuring classroom activities which may result in more meaningful education for children and youth
2. To enable the teacher to do more creative teaching and use a greater variety of instructional media
3. To enable the teacher to develop effective programs focusing upon the individual needs of students
4. To provide increased time for individualizing instruction, evaluating learning situations, student counseling and

guidance, and for other instructional activities that will improve educational opportunities for children

5. To relieve teachers of the numerous semi- and nonprofessional tasks which through the years have become cumulative and which have come to consume a disproportionate amount of the teacher's time and energies

IMPROVEMENT OF INSTRUCTION

It is obvious that the introduction of a teacher aide into an elementary classroom helps create a more supportive and encouraging environment for learning, resulting in greater achievement by children. Likewise, there is considerable evidence that there is a positive relationship between the utilization of aides in the classroom and higher scores on achievement tests.

A recent study by Nelson D. Crandall (October, 1970; *California State Board Journal*) investigated the effect of teacher aides on teacher behavior in the classroom. Crandall presented five conclusions:

1. When the aide is in the room, the teacher tends to spend a significantly greater percentage of time in small group work.
2. Teachers working with aides do use more supportive verbal expressions than when working alone. On a scale of seven classifications of expression (support, helping, receptive, routine, inattentive, unresponsive, disapproval), there was a marked weighting toward the supportive end of the scale.
3. Teachers working with an aide demonstrate more differences nonverbally than when working alone. Free from the necessity of pointing the finger, giving the evil eye, or placing the restraining hand on the shoulder, the teachers were much more nonverbally supportive than when working alone.
4. Teachers working with an aide use different frequencies and a greater range of methods than when working alone. They lecture and demonstrate less, they are much more

likely to give directions to an individual child, to ask questions in problem-solving situations, and to encourage the youngster to draw his own conclusions.

5. In the realm of cognition, teachers are apparently less inclined to be superficial in their treatment of subject matter when they have the help of an aide. (Cognition is defined as knowledge.) While most teacher talk remained at the knowledge and comprehension level, there was nonetheless a measurable and significant shift toward the more abstract cognitive levels.

It is also necessary for teachers to recognize the variety of contributions different individuals are able to make to the education of children. At one point or another, all learning experiences require some sort of adult direction, facilitation, and supervision. Whether the assistance should be provided by teachers or aides depends on the tasks themselves, the needs of children, and the skills of the people involved.

LEGAL IMPLICATIONS

Due to the comparatively recent use of the teacher aides, their function in our educational system is ill defined. There are no concrete definitions or measures of established practice which state and local school districts can use as guidelines. As of now, most states do not have specific statutory provisions pertaining to teacher aides. The majority of the school districts operating aide programs are doing so under general legislative provisions for operating and maintaining public school systems.

In recent years some state legislatures have enacted statutes providing for the employment of teacher aides. Some of these laws provide for teacher aides for specific purposes, while others are rather comprehensive and provide only a legal and broad-scale basis for such employment.

Other state boards of education and state departments of education have published statements concerning the use of aides in their public schools. Generally, these provisions have not been adopted as official state regulations and do not carry the weight of law, but they do lend guidance and direction in the employment and utilization of teacher aides.

In any consideration of an aide program, the question of authority and liability becomes very important. All states have certification laws which require persons to meet certain minimal qualifications before they may become teachers in the schools. Therefore, unless there are statutes that cover teacher aides, an aide is not authorized to substitute for a certificated teacher or become involved in the area of discipline matters.

Further, when teacher aides are assigned tasks involving supervision of children, they could be placed in positions of potential liability for pupil injury, unless specific policies give the aide the same protection afforded student teachers and regular teachers. Since most of the proposed aide programs involve job duties under the direct supervision of a teacher or team of teachers, the question of liability should not present a problem.

At the classroom level, teachers would be well advised to make certain that aides know the scope of their duties and responsibilities. It would be advisable, too, if teacher aides were provided instruction on how to deal with common situations such as, for example, misbehavior by children, student injury, and questions of responsibilities children may or may not assume. For the protection of children, aides should have a thorough knowledge of their own rights, authority, and responsibilities. With a minimum of foresight and a generous supply of common sense, teachers can prevent any legal problems from arising.

SELECTING TEACHER AIDES

While classroom teachers are seldom involved in the initial stages of the employment process for aides, some opportunities for input into the process are becoming available to teachers. For example, an experienced staff member may be given her choice of several different aides already employed by the district. Or, some teachers may be asked to recommend for employment parents and interested citizens who live within the school community. Increasingly, classroom teachers are being given an opportunity to make periodic evaluations of their aides, and in some districts, they are called upon to recommend reemployment. Regardless of the degree of current involvement, you should be prepared to lend your assistance whenever the opportunity arises.

It is imperative that attention be given to the qualifications aides who work in elementary school classrooms should possess and the duties they should perform. An aide, unfortunately, can be no better than her qualifications permit. The employment of aides with poor qualifications can be detrimental to the education of children. For example, since children learn much by emulating adults, an aide who exemplifies undesirable behavior might be doing children more harm than good.

Applicants for classroom aide positions should meet standards that will insure that they have the ability to perform the duties required. Selection for employment should be based on established criteria. A major factor to be considered is how well the applicant relates to and works with people, especially children. Also, consideration of the degree of "direct contact and experience with children" should be of primary importance in selecting a teacher aide. Additional criteria might well include the following:

- Average intelligence
- The ability to establish and maintain rapport with others
- Punctuality in meeting responsibilities
- Ability to speak clearly and distinctly
- Enthusiastic attitude
- Familiarity with general classroom procedures
- Knowledge of clerical procedures
- Resourcefulness in conducting activities related to the teaching process
- Ability to maintain discipline
- Emotional stability

It should also be remembered that the duties as well as the abilities of teacher aides differ. Some prefer to work with other groups of adults, some want to interact with children, and some are perfectly happy working in isolation. Distinctions can also be made between those who want limited responsibilities and those who hope to gradually increase their level of responsibility. Thus, while knowledge of professional ethics or the ability to relate well to people or to set a role example may be related to a teacher aide's success, such criteria may also be totally irrelevant.

ORIENTATION

Both teachers and aides should be given some solid orientation to skills and expectations before a teacher aide program is even launched. Teachers themselves must go through a process of role evaluation prior to embarking on the successful use of an aide. Someone has suggested that the teacher and aide ask themselves the following questions as a means of "lubricating" the process by which they work out their roles. Is the task at hand valid for children? Is it a valid learning experience for the aide? Does the task increase the responsibility of children? Are both the child and the aide comfortable with and qualified for the task?

While the teacher aide may attend in-service training classes to learn some skills that will be helpful in the classroom, the bulk of her orientation falls on the shoulders of the classroom teacher. The aide must adjust to your way of doing things in order to serve you well. Since you are the one who will be giving the directions, the opportunity to participate in the orientation of your aide might well be considered a privilege, for this enables you to produce your own "custom-made assistant." During this orientation period every effort should be made to develop a warm team relationship and an environment which encourages harmony and cooperation.

Recognizing your important role in training aides, you should give serious thought to the kind of orientation that will best facilitate an aide's growth. To a large degree, your aide's success will hinge on your ability to generate a viable program. For example, several months before the aide is scheduled to begin work, you could invite her to spend a day to share information and ideas. This simple procedure can serve to reduce many of the anxieties held by both you and the aide. At the

same time, you will have an opportunity to provide her with
materials, such as board of education policies and the teacher's
handbook, with which she should become familiar. Most aides
indicate that exposure to written guidelines is of real value to
them.

When the aide arrives for the preschool orientation work-
shop, she will be looking to you for advice, help, and guidance,
and it is your responsibility to supply them. Chances are that
she will be confused and insecure about what is ahead for her.
Anything you can do to minimize this will contribute much to
her success in your classroom. Take your aide under your wing.
Tour the school with her if the principal has not already done
so. Plan an extensive building excursion noting the following
people, places, and things:

People — Principal and assistants, school secretary, counselor, school psychologist, librarian, custodian,
nurse, cafeteria director, and other teacher aides

Places — Library, supply room, storage areas, workroom,
bookstore, conference rooms, cafeteria, audito-
rium, and teachers' lounge

Things — Audiovisual equipment, storage cabinets, and duplicating equipment

When the building tour is completed, you can focus on experiences for the aide within your own classroom. For example,
talk about your classroom and students, your own hopes and
anxieties — sharing leads to an open relationship. Provide a
table or desk for your aide. It is a way of saying, "This is your
classroom, too." If possible, obtain copies of textbooks and
curriculum guides, a dictionary, pads and pencils, etc., for her
use alone. Be sure she has a copy of all school schedules and
calendars. Take a few minutes to discuss the professional practices and standards of your school. If she is to be a member of
the staff, she must know what is expected of her.

By planning and implementing the kinds of activities already
discussed, you will enable your teacher aide to make a smoother
adjustment to the school building, the faculty, and your own
classroom. You may also want to plan ways to help your stu-

dents adjust to a teacher aide in their classroom. One important way this can be accomplished is to provide for early interaction between students and your aide.

PLANNING FOR PROFESSIONAL GROWTH

It is not intended that the aide's training should end with her orientation. When it comes to her professional growth, the best training ground is the school. Seeing is better than hearing, and doing is better than both. Many leading educators are of the opinion that the aide's program should have a natural laboratory — the classroom.

If teacher aides are to function effectively in educational programs, the professional staff must assume responsibility for assisting them in expanding their knowledge of children and their roles in increasing opportunities for learning by children. The usefulness of the aide should be restricted only by her own professional limitations. You should introduce the aide gradually to the skills and knowledge of her routine tasks and should help her gain new insights leading to the performance of additional tasks. Though you should avoid overwhelming your aide with floods of information, you should look beyond the clerical role so often assigned and let her experiment with duties more closely related to instruction.

It might be well to keep in mind that if aides have nothing to do but sit, they will just sit. Likewise, if they are not looking for anything, they probably will not find anything. Your job during these first days should be one of making the sitting a time of real observation — a time of "finding out" about the teaching-learning situation in your room. The aide can learn much about you, the pupils, and the classroom program from this observation. However, again, if she is not looking for anything as she observes, she probably will not learn anything. You have a responsibility to set purposes and point out the kinds of experiences that need the aide's attention during these observation periods.

Your aide will probably be anxious to examine the textbooks and other curriculum materials she will be using in assisting you in teaching. To make the examination of such materials as worthwhile as possible, be sure that you give her the teacher's edition of each of the books. It is important that her first contact with the texts be the teacher's editions because they explain the total program and purpose of the books.

As well as examining texts, your aide can profit from studying state curriculum guides, district courses of study, picture files, and audiovisual collections. Again, however, any help you can give her regarding "what to look for" will be helpful and make her examination of materials much more worthwhile than just a casual glance when she gets time.

One of the things a classroom assistant should experience during any training period is some directed reading in professional books and educational journals. The reading of professional materials will probably be most worthwhile when you assign them in such a way that the aide can see their applicability to something that is going on in the teaching-learning situation in your classroom. For example, if you have individualized instruction in your room, have the aide read a few articles or a chapter in a professional book on "individualized instruction." It might be a good idea to also suggest some reading on topics such as classroom management, discipline, homework, and grading.

Within the guidelines suggested above, the function of the aide is mutually worked out between the teacher and the aide. As a general rule of thumb, the instructional aide can perform any task not requiring professional training or judgment. Role definitions are developed in such a way as to consider the needs of individual teaching-learning situations. Flexibility should be the order of the day. It is not the purpose of a training program to create a rigid structure. The point is to utilize to the best advantage the unique talents of the individuals comprising the teaching-learning team.

The decision to have a teacher aide in your classroom implies a willingness on your part to provide the best possible experiences that will help the aide develop into an efficient and contributing member of the school's instructional team. It is often the classroom teacher's skill in organizing, skill in leadership, educational background, and philosophy of education which will ultimately determine the effectiveness of the classroom aide's experience in a given classroom.

STAFF RELATIONSHIPS

Most teachers welcome the addition of teacher aides to the staff. These teachers view teacher aides as partners in the task of educating children. Most teachers have spent their careers teaching alone in self-contained classrooms. They have not had to work closely with other adults. When faced with another adult, these teachers can become insecure or resentful of what they consider to be an intrusion in their classroom. This fear and resentment often has its source in past patterns of teacher assignments.

The school staff should show the aide due respect and help her in every professional way so she may contribute her maximum ability. The aide has the responsibility of showing staff members the respect and consideration due professional personnel.

In a similar manner the instructional aide is a team member of the school staff and must observe the confidential nature of such relationships. An aide will learn a great deal about each child in your room, and it is important that she does not discuss the children with whom she works except with the professional staff.

The aide should assist the teacher in implementing the prescribed program of instruction. She should recognize the position of leadership that must be maintained in teacher-pupil relationships. At no time should the aide commit an act or make any statement that will be detrimental to that position of leadership or to the teacher-pupil relationship. Teachers and aides should work closely together in enforcing school policies in regard to pupil discipline. At no time should the teacher aide assume the responsibility for determining and administering pupil punishment.

The following guidelines may be helpful in maintaining good teacher-teacher aide relationships:

1. Confer about assignments
2. Attend meetings together
3. Compliment each other about work that is well done (do not take each other for granted)
4. Increase the quality and quantity of the duties of the teacher aide as expertise grows

Although differences of opinion are common in any organization, conflicts between teachers and aides are destructive to the effective operation of a classroom and contrary to the purpose of a teacher aide program. Almost invariably, in a serious or prolonged conflict, the teacher aide must be transfered to another teacher. However, every effort should be made by both the teacher and aide to resolve the differences and to reestablish a smooth relationship. The welfare of children should be the ultimate determinant for retaining or releasing any teacher or aide.

Further, the teacher is responsible for conferring with parents and maintaining an open channel of communication with the family. The teacher aide should not interfere with this function. In special circumstances where you feel that the teacher aide can be of assistance, the aide may be invited to participate in the parent-teacher conference.

The role of the teacher aide should command the respect and obedience of the students. A warm relationship, established through mutual respect, should exist between pupils and the teacher aide. This will create a good climate for learning. If misconduct occurs under the supervision of the aide, she may reprimand but not punish. In problem cases, the classroom aide should refer the offender to the teacher for disciplinary action. The decision to send disciplinary cases to the principal is made by the teacher, not the teacher aide.

Finally, if the aide is to work for several different teachers, the staff should outline a policy for communication between the classroom teachers and the aide so that one teacher does not become possessive of one particular aide. In addition, it is usually a good idea, at least in the beginning, to have the assignments of aides channeled through a third party, such as an aide coordinator or the principal. As aides become more numerous, one of the experienced aides can be given the responsibility of supervising and making assignments for other aides. This communications procedure can eliminate friction between teachers when they begin to depend upon the aides for routine duties.

DEVELOPING A PROPER PROFESSIONAL IMAGE

The exposure your teacher aide gets to your attitude and behavior will be very important in terms of her own professional development. If she is to view teaching as a profession, then she should see teachers behaving as professional people. Everything that you say and do will help to mold the kind of professional person your aide ultimately becomes. The image you project in the classroom and elsewhere in the school will probably become the image that will make the most impact on your aide. Projecting the proper professional image may be one of the most demanding tasks you will have as you work with an aide in your classroom.

Sometime during the first few weeks you should expose your new professional aide to some of the professional ethics and practices which we profess to follow in education. When possible, you might want to post a copy of the "Code of Ethics of the Teaching Profession." Codes can usually be obtained from your local education association or from some other teachers' professional organization. Your own school district may even have some printed material available on the subject. If your district has such material available in a handbook, you may choose to make the topic part of one of your conferences with your aide. While you can help your aide best by setting a good example, she will probably also profit from any material you can furnish and any discussion you can have on the subject.

As in all professions, there is always a certain amount of "shop talk" necessary as teachers work together daily to get a job done. You must realize, however, that your aide is going to be impressionable as she begins to work with you and other teachers. Unfortunately, she will probably not be "hardened" to most of the realities and frustrations that you have learned to cope with over the years. You may need to concentrate on talking about ideas rather than individuals as you get involved in education "shop talk." Discuss children in a manner that will command her respect for your ability to conduct business on a professional level. The manner in which you comment about students and other staff members will be closely observed by your new aide. As you discuss "shop talk" show compassion and respect for individuals. If it becomes necessary for you to discuss a problem of a personal nature, do it someplace and sometime without the aide present.

One further suggestion should be given to teachers who supervise aides. While the aide will usually find much enjoyment in the faculty room or lounge, it is not uncommon for aides to abuse its use from time to time. When this happens, do her a favor. Tell her your feelings about it. She needs to learn how to use the faculty room, and you can help her. It is not a hangout or a rest station. Instead, it needs to be respected as a room in which professional people can relax and discuss mutual concerns. Again, your example will be very important. You can teach her to enjoy the faculty lounge by using it properly yourself.

Also remember that as well as measuring your professionalism by the way you work with children and other teachers, the aide will measure your professionalism by the way you work with her.

EVALUATING AIDE EFFECTIVENESS

Closely allied to professional growth is the measurement and evaluation of teacher aide effectiveness. While the emphasis in assessment should be on self-appraisal and staff involvement, those individuals responsible for directing aide activities should be cognizant of the contribution that teacher aide evaluation can make to the assessment of professional growth needs. This contribution will be worthwhile to the extent that teacher aide evaluation can be conducted fairly and properly.

The teacher aide, as such, is a paraprofessional. She cannot make curriculum decisions, nor can she make decisions related to programming for specific students. The aide can only act as an extension of the certified educator who makes such decisions. Supervision by the classroom teacher can take several forms. The teacher should closely observe the enactment of her instructions by the aide. This observation will assure the teacher that the teacher aide is performing that which the teacher would have performed. Supervision by the teacher should also be given to those activities which the teacher aide conducts after being given verbal or written directions by the teacher.

This is not to assume that the aide is not trustworthy. Rather, it is a reaction to the realization that only the teacher may make decisions in regard to student discipline, effective learning climate, and content presented within the classroom. Because the teacher is responsible for the final actions of the aide, the teacher must be constantly informed as to the aide's process and progress with direct assignments.

A major difficulty in aide evaluation is that we educators have not been able to come to an agreement on which areas and competencies should be evaluated. However, there is little argument with the fact that the purpose of the evaluation will strongly influence the areas which are chosen for evaluation as well as the methods which will be used in the evaluation. The purposes for which we evaluate teacher aides are manifold. Generally speaking, we can divide the purposes into two broad categories. First, there is evaluation for administrative purposes, which is designed to gather information likely to assist administrators and teachers making decisions. Secondly, there is instructional evaluation which has as its primary purpose the improvement of the teaching-learning process. This is the type of evaluation that is done with the hope that better teaching and learning will result.

In addition, there are at least three views on how instructional evaluation can contribute to professional growth. First, there is the view that if aides are evaluated, they are motivated to do a more effective job. The idea behind this view is that most individuals need a little goading, a little pressure, or a little urging in order to exert themselves to perform better than just adequately. However, evaluation, of itself, will not provide the aide with the necessary assistance needed for change. Rather, evaluation must be a starting point for both personal and professional growth.

A second view is that evaluation should help the teacher assist the aide to do a better job in the instructional process. This view is particularly valid and applicable in the case of new aides who need help with basic instructional techniques. At the very least, this form of evaluation should provide teachers with factual information in regard to instructional needs of teacher aides.

A third viewpoint is that evaluation should stimulate aides' self-evaluation of their instructional capabilities. This view has the virtue of recognizing that no one except the aide can improve or change herself. Other staff members may assist a classroom assistant in making improvements, in encouraging her to change, or even in bringing force to bear on her to change; yet, whatever change takes place in an aide must be of her own doing. Change will take place when she decides it is important to change, when she perceives a need for change, and when she understands what the nature of the change ought to be.

Finally, continuous evaluation of teacher aide effectiveness helps to insure that aides will seek to improve the quality of their classroom performance. The procedures used should be tailored to the educational philosophy and curriculum emphasis of the entire staff. If evaluation is based upon a mutually accepted plan, is aide centered, and follows morale-building procedures, it should stimulate aides to produce a better teaching-learning climate and lead to self-criticism and self-improvement.

SUMMARY

Educators are in agreement that teacher aides have a vital role to play in making the teaching process more manageable. Despite the overall endorsement of the teacher's need for assistance, how well these assistants will serve teachers and pupils will depend on how they are utilized. Job analysis studies have shown that from 21 to 69 percent of the teacher's time is spent in performing tasks which do not require a high degree of professional competence. Hence, the need is demonstrated for more efficient use of the professional competence of the teacher.

Day-to-day supervision of the aide is the responsibility of the teacher, and it is important that there be complete understanding between the teacher and the aide as to the proper role of each in the classroom. In addition, the teacher aide should be equipped with enough knowledge and skills to make her job a pleasant and rewarding task. Such training helps the instructional assistant become acquainted with the work situation and learn her responsibilities.

Teachers working with aides must rely upon their own judgment when assigning classroom duties to their nonprofessional helpers. The kind and quantity of work they will be able to do will depend on the competency of the aide and is left to the discretion of the teacher. Each teacher will find various ways to utilize her aide — increasing her duties as experience and teacher judgment command.

CHAPTER 2

WORKING WITH THE TEACHER AIDE

O N the first day of school each year thousands of teachers and teacher aides meet for the first time. Usually in such cases neither the aide nor the teacher is prepared for their meeting or knows how to work properly with the other person. This lack of preparation often leads to the inefficient use of both the instructional aide and the teacher. Much of this misunderstanding concerning the aide's role can be avoided if teachers are trained to effectively utilize aides.

However, teachers must remember that the training of instructional aides is at a much lower level than teacher training, and therefore they will need more guidance than even a new teacher. Since aides will play a supportive role, they should be considered as dependent, not independent, personnel. Explicit directions must be given, and teachers must not hesitate to direct aides when needed. However, it is important that all team members do not direct or demand at once. It is often much more effective to have one team member transmit or relay major demands or expectations rather than have four or five teachers giving directions.

Proficiency in any task results from practice. Aides must be trained in order to serve you well. If in the performance of their duties aides can add vigor to our educational system, the investment will be worth the effort.

MAKING YOUR EXPECTATIONS KNOWN

Free and open communication is of utmost importance in working with a teacher aide. It has been our experience that many problems can be avoided if effective communication between teacher and aide exists. Teachers must also appreciate the fact that they are asking someone else to do a task for them, and they have to accept the results. They should be aware that no one will do the job as they would and should be encouraged to be patient with aides.

Early in your working relationship you should make clear the expectations you hold for the aide. You may know in your own mind exactly what your criteria for success are — but your aide will never know unless you specify them. Such communication removes much of the guesswork and uncertainty commonly associated with being a teacher aide. Also, it is not uncommon for the classroom teacher to set her standards on the basis of the aide she had last year. It should be obvious that such comparisons are not always in the best interest of the parties involved. Recognizing the vast differences in abilities of individuals, it would be best to set your expectations in line with the capabilities of your present aide.

Some teachers have found it useful to communicate their expectations by means of a checklist or brief guide. You might want to share the following outlines with your new aide.

Suggestions for Improving Your Efficiency as an Aide

1. Learn the names of the pupils in your room as soon as possible.
2. Learn as much as you can about each pupil as quickly as possible.
3. Lend personal assistance to pupils whenever possible.
4. Give encouragement to pupils wherever and whenever you can.
5. Praise each pupil's efforts and success.
6. Be patient in dealing with pupils.
7. Consult often with the teacher as to how you can assist.
8. Learn the routine of the school day.
9. Become familiar with the school building, playground, etc.
10. Become acquainted immediately with emergency procedures.

Responsibilities of the Teacher Aide

1. Do I plan for the activity which I have been assigned — not hit or miss or just doing something?

2. Do I make myself helpful by offering my services to the teacher when there is an obvious need for help?
3. Do I observe closely so as to know children's likes, dislikes, preferences, enthusiasms, aversions, etc.?
4. Do I observe closely the techniques used by the teacher and follow through when I am working with the group?
5. Do I really listen to what the children have to say?
6. Do I evaluate myself at intervals?
7. Do I accept criticisms and suggestions without becoming emotionally upset?
8. Do I follow the directions of the classroom teacher?
9. Do I try to develop a friendly attitude with all of my co-workers?
10. Do I realize that my whole purpose for being in the classroom is to assist the teacher in order that the children might progress more rapidly?
11. Do I avoid criticism of the children, teacher, and the school?

A cordial relationship between the teacher and aide is considered essential. Be sure your directions are clear and that the aide understands what is expected of her. Be willing to teach the aide skills she can learn and wants to learn. Include the reason for assigning the task as well as the "how to do it" information.

A good deal of the success of a classroom teacher depends upon human relations. In this particular case success depends upon the degree of effectiveness with which you can relate to your teacher aide. Many teacher aides have complained in the past that they have not been given enough responsibility. You need to examine and explore those managerial skills essential for working with a classroom aide such as scheduling, sharing responsibilities, and using time, space, and resources effectively. Are you willing to let your aide assume challenging responsibilities as well as the routine ones?

SITTING DOWN TO TALK

Conferences between the teacher and the aide are a vital part of the growth experiences of both. These meetings should be held at regular intervals during the school year, and specific purposes for these sessions should be established. The aide really needs to know how she is doing. Since the financial rewards for noncertificated personnel are so far below that of the professional staff, you must go the "extra mile" when it comes to providing evaluation feedback to your aide. At the least, your expression of confidence will help the aide renew her energy and be better prepared to attack upcoming experiences with vigor.

Of course, aides will make mistakes from time to time just as teachers do. It is imperative that you discuss areas in need of improvement soon after they become visible. Not only should you discuss these mistakes, but together with your aide you should agree on strategies to correct the situation. The failure to develop a well-conceived plan of attack to bring needed change has caused the demise of many an aide's job.

What meaningful subjects could be discussed during these sessions? It is a simple matter to write down questions and concerns that come to mind as you work with your aide. These can then be brought up in a scheduled conference at a later date.

Conferences should be used to review the aide's progress, to clear up uncertainties, and to plan. The teacher should not do all of the talking. The only time a teacher needs to point something out to an aide is when the aide cannot see it herself. Objective observation techniques and frequent postobservation conferences make for a more meaningful relationship between the teacher and the aide.

Teachers may wish to devise their own system for recording certain aide behaviors or interactions. It is often a good idea to gather data on an aide's questioning skills, for instance. A very simple classification of questions into two categories, such as (1) open questions and (2) closed questions, could allow a teacher to easily record the kinds of questions an aide is using. An open question would be one which calls for a multiword answer and which opens a subject up for extended discussion. A closed question would be one which calls for a *yes* or *no* answer.

Armed with objective data gathered during several observations, the teacher is now in a position to have a meaningful conference with her aide. She can report that the aide used open questions 70 percent of the time during three observations. This means much more on an evaluation than merely saying, "You handled class questioning well (or not so well)."

It is recommended that a conference be held early in the aide's work experience. This will allow the aide to intelligently modify her behavior. Too often, teachers register their dislikes only on the final "written evaluation" — after it is too late. Again, there is wisdom in communicating early and often.

The rapport you develop with your teacher aide will determine, to a great extent, the success of your conference. You will need to build a rapport in which there is sincerity, warmth, sensitivity, and respect. Rapport must be built. You will be able to do your part in building rapport through consistent attention to the following kinds of behavior:

1. Treat your aide with respect in your dealings with her.
2. Share the workload.
3. Do not permit the conference to drift into a question-and-answer period.
4. Be on time for conferences and come prepared for any discussion.
5. Do not correct the teacher aide in the presence of others.

As you strive to develop rapport and also endeavor to establish worthwhile conference topics, you may want to spend some time evaluating your own work with your aide. Occasionally, a good working relationship may seem to be slow in developing, and conferences may seem to be a worthless exercise. When this happens, you may want to ask yourself some of the following questions:

1. Did I carefully orient the aide to her required tasks?
2. Did I clearly state what assistance I expect from the teacher aide in sharing classroom duties with me?
3. Did I give the aide opportunities to show her initiative

and creative ability?

4. Did I give my criticism in a positive and constructive manner?

5. Am I doing all I can to develop the aide's feeling of security and to promote good rapport between the aide and myself?

When a conference has terminated, the wise teacher should carefully review her notes and mentally check through the conference results to assess her effectiveness as a counselor and problem solver. In this process she should review what went "wrong," what went "right," and reflect on what she can do in the next conference to improve her effectiveness. Some teachers enjoy writing a self-evaluation report and periodically referring to this report to gauge the progress made in subsequent conferences.

DELEGATING ASSIGNMENTS

As soon as an aide program begins to function effectively and teachers begin to reap the rewards of this additional help, they may have a tendency to overestimate an aide's ability. Quite often teachers give more and more of their own responsibilities to the aide and may begin to delegate assignments that should be carried out by the teacher. In matching the tasks at hand with the capabilities of the aide involved, teachers must also concern themselves with the job satisfaction of those working directly under their supervision. Too often, teacher aides quit out of frustration.

No doubt part of the problem lies in the tasks aides are asked to perform. Although classroom aides can and should provide a wide variety of services, they are often asked to do what teachers themselves would be unwilling to do. How many teachers, for instance, would knowingly volunteer to run a duplicating machine or collate papers for fifteen hours a week?

In order to effectively introduce your aide to classroom duties it will be necessary for you to have an overall plan. Begin by assigning her simple initial tasks and move her into increasingly more complex assignments later. Regardless of the aide's apparent competence, she should begin with a simple clerical or housekeeping task. She should not be given several tasks at once, nor should she immediately be assigned to work directly with students. The only exceptions to this rule would be such simple chores as distributing paper, scissors, or crayons to students. In addition, she should not be given complicated book-keeping tasks or the responsibility for money collection.

After an aide has demonstrated her ability to effectively handle simple tasks, such as duplicating materials or distributing paper work, she may be given more complicated assignments. For example, after grading sets of simple papers, she may be assigned the task of marking longer sets of homework papers or grading more involved objective test papers. Likewise, after successfully working with one student as a tutor, she may graduate to working with a child in a remedial situation. From this one-to-one assignment a competent aide can gradually move on to work with a small group of children in a supervisory capacity.

Aides as well as teachers need to feel that their work is necessary and appreciated. They need to enjoy what they are doing. It is largely the responsibility of the classroom teacher to help aides see themselves as important members of the teaching family. The aide should be accepted as a "partner" by the teacher and become involved in the totality of the learning situation. Planning and operation of all classroom activities should be developed and handled through close relationship and combined effort. Division of duties, both professional and nonprofessional, should be established on a daily and long-term basis and premised to a large degree on the interests and abilities of each person. The teacher must remain as the classroom leader but should treat the "partner" in a near-peer relationship to the point that the aide is encouraged to participate in all classroom activities where competency may be expected or developed.

Basic guidelines are needed to help insure appropriate and economical use of an aide's time. Generally speaking, tasks that require the most professional skills should be reserved for those with the most professional training. All too often, an aide, regardless of training, is thought of as someone to work with the slow learner, the "bottom group," or children with learning disabilities. Yet, there is a basic contradiction in expecting a person with little or no professional training to succeed where teachers with four or five years of professional training have not.

Within the duties that the teacher aide can be expected to perform the teacher should attempt in all possible ways to provide a gamut of total exposure to activities for the aide. That is to say that the aide's services should be divided into the three areas of clerical, instructional, and administrational. A balanced work day will provide the aide with a variety of experiences supportive of the total educational program. It has been our experience that in the aide programs which have been deemed most unsatisfactory, teachers, aides, and administrators alike have, in most cases, centered their grievances around an unbalanced work load for the teacher aide. While utilizing her aide the classroom teacher must be fully aware of the range of opportunities that can be provided for the aide as well as the possible negative by-products which can result from assigning an unbalanced work load to the aide.

STRENGTHENING LEADERSHIP

Teachers vary in their expectations of aides. Sometimes they make unreasonable demands; at other times, teachers set requirements well below the capacities of teacher aides. To avoid this, you should make a realistic analysis of the potential strengths and weaknesses of your aide and pattern your expectations accordingly. Generally, you will do well to set high standards and count on your aide to attain them. Individuals tend to respond more favorably when much is expected of them rather than too little.

Most staff members prefer the quality of consistency in leadership behavior. However, this does not mean they appreciate the teacher who undertakes listless or unimaginative actions. Rather, they appreciate an individual who pursues a style of leadership undergirded by basic principles and characterized by well-planned and carefully carried out actions.

There are certain principles relating to leadership that should be second nature to the teacher who supervises teacher aides. These principles must be manifested in the actions of any teacher who expects to obtain the maximum effectiveness from her aide. First, the teacher must be a coordinator. She must determine what is most important and establish a priority list of those things that are necessary for the success of the educational program. She must fit everybody together and coordinate many diverse activities so that they make sense and are logical to her aide. Second, the teacher must learn to be sensitive to the needs of individuals. As the teacher learns to be sensitive to people, she is in effect becoming aware of their needs and differences. Third, the teacher should have imagination and be willing to promote experimentation. Conditions are constantly changing. The teacher should encourage her aide to experiment with materials and methods. Finally, the teacher must communicate. Her aide needs to be kept informed. Lack of information breeds misunderstanding. Valuable time is lost clarifying issues which would not have arisen had adequate communication existed.

The teacher who practices sound personnel management procedures usually does not have to worry about respect from her teacher aide. Generally, she will be held in high esteem. In such circumstances she attains respect naturally and readily. If opposite circumstances prevail, no amount of demanding will produce respect.

Further, the teacher who reverses herself without notice, who is cold and insensitive one day and warm and solicitous the next merely keeps staff members on edge and uncomfortable. If aides know what is expected from the teacher and can be certain about her expectations, they are more able to adjust their own behavior patterns accordingly.

The teacher who displays effective personnel management practices will do the following:

1. Capitalize on the professional and personal strengths of a teacher aide.

2. Maintain high performance standards and encourage their fulfillment
3. Make working conditions as optimal as possible
4. Strive for consistency in supervisory behavior
5. Organize the classroom in a manner that promotes good order and a sense of forward movement
6. Distribute duties in a fair and equitable manner

INCREASING AIDES' EFFECTIVENESS

Helping aides, both new and experienced, on the job is definitely related to good personnel management procedures. If the classroom teacher has a voice in selecting the aide for her room, this responsibility starts before the aide is even assigned.

During the process of orientation and introduction, handling matters vital to the adjustment of new aides is, as already indicated, definitely within the realm of your responsibility.

Helping the aide on the job has many facets which overlap and commingle with each other. Since aides, unlike teachers, are not the product of an extensive preparation program, a significant proportion of their skills may be acquired through imitation of the teachers. In the beginning, at least, you may have to do a great deal of preliminary planning together with your aide, but as time passes things should be easier. In addition, the aide should come to know the students as individuals — their specific needs, interests, and abilities. Informal feedback and brainstorming sessions with other staff members and supervisors should be helpful for the aide in gaining new insights.

Be sensitive to areas that need improvement. Some of these areas may include working conditions, physical facilities, and organizational structure. When a change in material matters or conditions is possible, make every effort to bring about the desirable change. If the area in need of change relates to nontangible things, such as interpersonal relationships, you may find it more difficult to institute corrective actions. Yet, you should make an attempt to improve the situation. Sincere concern, followed by a reasonable action, will do much to improve your aide's morale and keep it high.

For example, small things often have a major bearing upon morale. Give recognition to your aide for a job well done. Be sensitive to poor working conditions or to some physical deficiency. When an aide feels that the teacher cares about what is going on and that she is sensitive to the daily activities and concerns of her aide, she feels better able to endure less than optimum working conditions.

While you cannot eliminate all of the impediments to the adjustment of new aides, you can and should anticipate as many difficulties as possible. Here are some specific suggestions:

1. Let the aide know where and how to find help when it is needed. Half the battle is knowing where to go for help.
2. Enlist the cooperation of experienced instructional aides in helping new aides to adjust. Many elementary schools have used a "helping" aide or an arrangement of pairing each new aide with a warm and cooperative experienced aide.
3. Show the new aide that you are concerned about her adjustment and development. Since new personnel are often reluctant to admit they are having difficulty, you may need to provide help in as unobtrusive a manner as possible.
4. Aides want to know what is expected of them. They need to know that their own understanding fits the job description you have for their position. Furthermore, the aide will feel better and perform better knowing that her teacher is aware of her problems and her needs.

The quality of service rendered by classroom aides is directly related to their sense of belonging to a team and the awareness of their importance to this team. Each member must recognize and respect the role of the other before the degree of cooperation and teamwork necessary for the smooth operation of the classroom can be attained. Each must be dedicated to the total job to be performed and feel her task is a vital one.

ADMINISTERING CONSTRUCTIVE CRITICISM

Offering constructive criticism without arousing resentment may be considered a fine art in the field of human relations. Very few supervisors are able to master this art. The problem is that all of us have a desire to protect the ego, or self. In all of us there is a great deal of vanity. Therefore it is difficult for most of us to accept constructive criticism with grace.

Criticism is most effective when it is done in a relaxed manner. Experienced supervisors have found this task to be one of the most important keys to effective leadership. It is not necessary to criticize severely in order to obtain results. Such criticism does more harm than good. When it becomes necessary to give constructive criticism, you should not do so without careful prior planning. You must remember this: the purpose of criticism is neither to show anger, nor to punish, nor to create unhappiness. The purpose is to help the individual to understand what can be improved and to make her anxious to do better.

Constructive criticism, to be effective, should be softened with praise. This praise must, of course, be deserved. Before anyone is criticized, time must be taken to appreciate positive aspeacts of the individual's performance. Criticism is much easier to take when there is a good deal of praise mixed into the recipe.

Before offering suggestions for the solution of a problem, the aide should be given an opportunity to criticize herself. The subject should probably be brought up in an incidental manner. Remember that a good technique is to bring up the subject and see what the aide thinks about it. If she is aware of the need for improvement she may prefer to admit her shortcomings, at least to herself, rather than have the teacher point them out.

When offering constructive criticism the teacher must use due caution. She must not seem to act superior or appear insincere. All human beings make mistakes. Just remember that teacher performance is often somewhat short of perfect.

Teachers can set an example by recognizing their own mistakes and correcting them as promptly as possible.

In discussing a particular point with an aide you should recall having made a similar error yourself. One cannot turn a poor worker into a good one by whipping her with words. Criticism must aim at the goals of good will and improved performance. Criticism should be used to assist the aide, not to punish her.

HELPING AIDES TO UNDERSTAND AND GUIDE CHILDREN

The classroom aide who is unable to understand the behavior of children may well find herself in an awkward situation. The teacher who does not effectively help her aide to develop a better understanding of the nature of children will find herself in the position of correcting a problem that should not have occurred. Such a problem can leave everyone defeated and discouraged.

The teacher who can effectively help aides to develop a better understanding of children will find that fewer problems arise, enabling both to devote more time and energy to teaching. Helping the aide to bridge the gap from exasperation to satisfaction should be one of the primary goals of the teacher. Your attitude is of the utmost importance since it sets the pace and can spell success or failure. Most teachers have found that a positive approach will encourage the classroom aide while a negative approach may well stifle initiative and creativity.

Most of the descriptions of the ideal qualities of a classroom aide carry the prerequisite, "She must like children." Liking children means having a willingness to listen. Listening is more than nodding your head as you continue whatever activity is occurring when the interruption occurs. It means that the aide does stop and listen and respond in an appropriate manner. Listening to children requires a sincere interest in what they have to say. A sincere interest requires an understanding of the child, his interest level, the nature of his curiosity, his sense of humor, the problems he faces, and the dimensions of his world.

Aides should understand that the modern elementary school is more than just a place where youngsters are taught subject matter and skills. One of the primary objectives of education today is to assist the individual to a happier, more productive, and more satisfying life. The school, therefore, must recognize and provide for the individual differences which are manifested in the school's population.

There is a real need for school personnel to cultivate the habit of seeing the behavior of children as the most important clue to understanding children. The social needs of children are deep-seated and powerful motivators of behavior. Security in social relationships is a need that influences all that people are and all that they do. Certainly there is a positive relationship between the teacher's and aide's understanding of children and the quality of the classroom environment.

Observation and listening are basic ingredients in all techniques which develop the aide's understanding of children. There are various ways that teachers can help aides to improve their observation techniques. Some have suggested that teachers and aides watch children whose responses to situations are inappropriate and, if they subscribe to the belief that every response must have a cause, seek out that cause. School situations provide a wide variety of opportunities for the observation of the students. For instance, the observation of children at play generally provides valuable insights into the behavior of children and is often used by child guidance clinics. Much of the same insight can be derived by the aide from study of the particular item which the student draws, writes, models, or represents dramatically.

Learning to describe behavior objectively sharpens the aide's awareness of how subjective we really are in our daily observations. As she becomes familiar with the technique of objective evaluation, the aide will discover that it is possible to accept and understand a child without judging him. Aides should be encouraged to listen to children as they express themselves without trying to impose their own thinking and feelings upon them. An aide who spends too much time talking will have little time to study behavior. Being a good listener is one of the best ways to maintain clear channels of communication.

Aides working on the playground may sometimes watch student activities by looking only for signs of trouble instead of looking also for positive behavior. Posture, laughter, tears, and voice pitch are just a few factors that may indicate health problems or emotional strain that need further investigation. When an aide is aware of these factors she can enlist the aid of the teacher and playground director for some really purposeful observation.

Increasingly, elementary schools are obtaining specialists to help teachers understand and plan for students more adequately. These specialists, through diagnostic and therapeutic procedures, assist student adjustment and educational planning. Maximum aid is given to teachers and aides — when each resource person is able to work as a member of a team.

The classroom teacher can help her aide to better understand students by setting the example with her own attitude and activities. The studies she encourages, the training she gives, the creative ideas to which she is receptive can mean the difference between personnel that merely work and personnel that work with that extra spark because they know their work is meaningful, is functional, and is appreciated. The aide who gives herself a chance, making that extra effort to do better and to know a little more, and the teacher who encourages and helps her both by word and example will make a teaching team that will be hard to beat.

CLASSROOM MANAGEMENT

Closely allied to understanding children is the process of classroom management. An aide soon learns that familiarity with subject matter and knowledge of teaching techniques are not all that are demanded of an elementary school teacher. As a matter of fact, other responsibilities and duties seem to require much of her attention, such as collecting lunch money, keeping attendance records, maintaining a neat and attractive classroom, and distributing and collecting materials. To ignore these tasks, even though they may seem menial and possibly unpleasant, would bring chaos and unhappiness into the classroom environment. A teacher must recognize the necessity of a well-managed classroom and try to provide one that is attractive and comfortable. An aide can assist in providing more opportunities to teach and a better environment in which children can learn.

An interesting and eventful classroom is one variable which the teacher and aide can manipulate. The classroom should attract the children to it. The pictures, plants, animals, and learning corner should stimulate children's questions, curiosity, or need to learn. The place for a child to learn should be an environment which informs children.

Through the teacher's and aide's examples, classroom courtesy and politeness may be taught. The aide who displays a courteous attitude toward children is encouraging them to be courteous, not only to adults but to the other children in the room. If the aide learns each child's name as soon as possible, this can add to both classroom control and courtesy.

Poor management on the part of a teacher during the roll call or the collection of lunch money can cause behavioral problems in the classroom. However, those routine tasks of taking attendance and accounting for children who will be eating in the school cafeteria could be assumed by an aide, thus freeing the teacher for more important tasks.

Some teachers have rather strict regulations concerning children wandering around the classroom. Other teachers find that it is not necessary to have such regulations. Problems that can result when children are moving about the classroom can be eliminated before they exist if the teacher and aide are constantly aware of each child at all times. If the aide is continually alert to what is happening in the classroom, she is prepared to give extra help at a trouble spot and thus eliminate a behavior problem.

In addition, teachers should avoid having to waste their time or the aide's time searching for equipment and materials. All classroom equipment, supplies, and teaching devices should be kept in a specific place. An aide can help you keep classroom drawers and closets in order. A well-ordered closet or drawer makes it easier to select and return teaching equipment. A simple procedure to follow is to have shelves in the drawers and closets labeled so as to identify the items contained in each.

Finally, the teacher should expect her aide to assist with the management of materials within her classroom. Materials collection, distribution, and preparation are all necessarily planned activities in which the classroom aide can be involved. Materials that are essential for the day's activity should be prepared and be ready for use at the time the activity begins. Children waiting for materials can create behavior problems. Much of the teacher's time and energy can be saved if aides are utilized to organize and distribute materials and supplies in a businesslike, preplanned system.

THE TEACHER AIDE AND DISCIPLINE

The beginning aide usually encounters her first problems on the job in the area of classroom control or "discipline." In most cases disciplinary situations can be easily avoided by thorough educational planning and proper implementation. Teacher aides cannot be expected to deal with many of the problems that will arise as they work with children. However, as aides work with individual children and small groups they may observe behavior that the classroom teacher does not see. Aides should be instructed to call to your attention any disturbing behavior they observe. You can then make a decision as to the seriousness of the problem and offer suggestions on ways of dealing with the situation. The aide should always act as follows:

1. Refer behavioral problems to the classroom teacher
2. Follow the teacher's suggestions for influencing the behavior of children
3. Regard all discussions of children as confidential

Make sure that the aide realizes there should be some consistency as the two of you work with the class. However, she will probably have a better initial instructional experience if you help her establish herself as a distinct personality. Any time the aide is working with a group of children she should have the responsibility and authority for maintaining control and discipline. Initially, teacher aides should be left alone with the entire class for only short periods of time. Later, when you leave the aide on her own, be sure that she knows where you are in case an emergency should arise.

The aim of good discipline should be to help the individual child adjust to the personal and social forces of his experiences. First, the child must learn to adjust to himself as a growing and developing individual. Second, the child must adjust to the existing culture and institutions in which he is a participant. Finally, he often will have to adjust the standards of his home environment to those of the school.

Prior to the aide's appearance in the classroom, you may want to think about how you control and discipline your students. What is the general noise level in your room? How much self-control do you expect the children to display? How do you help the students develop self-control? How "mature" are they? How do you discipline children who misbehave?

In some instances, you may wish to point out to your aide potential troublemakers as well as children who are generally helpful. In other cases, you may wish to let the teacher aide determine who the troublemakers are and who reacts well to her. Certainly, many behavioral problems are not the same from teacher to teacher even when the same child is involved in each case.

Nevertheless, the main purpose in teaching discipline is to prepare children to stand on their own, to take care of themselves, and to make their own decisions. If they are to make wise decisions, it is important that they be taught in ways that help them learn to think for themselves. The teacher aide can help with discipline by doing the following:

1. Showing the children that they are important; learning their names as soon as possible; listening to them and remembering things they tell her
2. Praising behavior she wants repeated
3. Explaining why some kinds of behavior are not acceptable

4. Showing the child that she is interested in helping him
5. Giving him words and sentences for explaining and showing emotions
6. Explaining reasons for doing things in a certain way
7. Encouraging the child to take part in planning an activity
8. Offering an alternative when giving an order to provide a choice for the child to make. This will permit him to act without just obeying or disobeying.

Students normally respond better to adults who show a personal interest in them. Aides should be encouraged to spend a portion of each class period developing individual relationships with students in the class. This is especially true at the beginning of the shool year. Likewise, personal knowledge of each child brings about a strengthened desire on the part of the teacher and the aide for greater tolerance and understanding and for improved individual educational planning. Misconduct can be better understood and more often tolerated when it is seen in the light of a child's emotional needs.

SUMMARY

Teacher aides perform a wide variety of tasks, many if not most of which are unique to each position. For this reason on-the-job training is extremely important. You should be aware that aides have a vital contribution to make; thus it becomes important for teachers and aides to learn to live and work together harmoniously and productively on behalf of the children. Every effort should be made to develop warm personal relationships and an environment which encourages harmony and cooperative effort.

Most teachers have always taken complete responsibility for their classrooms. They are not familiar, through experience or training, with assuming a mangerial capacity when an assistant becomes a member of the team, and it is difficult for them to delegate responsibilities to such an assistant. Nevertheless, the teacher-manager will need to evaluate the performance of aides as well as students. Misunderstandings will be avoided if the roles and functions of both teacher and aide are clearly understood. Teachers working with an aide must rely upon their own good judgment in assigning duties to their aide.

The quality of the relationship between teacher and aide will often depend upon the amount of time they spend together planning and organizing their activities in the classroom. Effective organization tends to reduce conflicts and improve the coordination and effectiveness of operations in the classroom.

CHAPTER 3

TEACHER AIDE UTILIZATION

THE presence of an aide in an elementary school classroom can make all the difference in the world in the amount of individual help children receive. One teacher alone, even the most capable, can cope with only so much going on all at once. Alone you have to limit the scope of activities, ignoring many experiences that would be significant, and put off those that require too much direct supervision. However, a team, the teacher and aide, can assist children with both the intellectual and emotional support they need when they need it.

When instructional aides are utilized in the classroom to improve and reinforce achievement in the basic skill areas, the results are often amazing. Achievement test results in language arts, mathematics, and science often show students gaining twice what they normally would in one academic year in a classroom without an aide. More than one teacher has pointed out that having a teacher aide is just like having another teacher in the class. By working with individuals and small groups the aide can help reinforce and refine the teacher's plan for instruction in the classroom.

In addition, there are many intangible assets that teacher aides bring to the classroom that cannot be measured by achievement tests. For example, the aide provides the teacher with a valuable associate for planning. As a result, planning and implementation can be done as a team enterprise. Also, the teacher aide often brings complementary talents to the classroom, such as the ability to play the piano, to paint, or to speak a foreign language. Further, an additional adult in the room can provide youngsters with another teacher figure with whom to identify. In fact, many students may find it much easier to relate to the teacher aide than to the teacher.

Outside the regular classroom, particularly on the playground, the aide can lend assistance to the teaching staff. She may be younger or more vigorous than the teacher and thus able to more energetically participate in the play of children. Or, the aide may have a background in athletics or physical education. This could make recess a more meaningful and productive experience for children.

The tasks that teacher aides perform, of course, will vary greatly from school to school and from classroom to classroom. What the aide does will depend on the needs of the school, the teacher, and the pupils as well as on the creativity of individual staff members. Even though aides are not expected to have either the skills or the professional training of classroom teachers, they can broaden the teacher's sphere of action. When provided with proper training, aides add a vital dimension to the instructional process. With a certified teacher as the team leader, classroom aides become vitally important, supportive members of the team.

However, schools have too often utilized teacher aides only as clerical assistants. This practice has led to a reexamination of the roles assigned to nonprofessional staff members. For example, should aides be given responsibility under teacher guidance for some instructional tasks? Should they work with individual students as tutors? Could they drill small groups of students in the mechanics of reading? Most educators agree that as the teacher aide staff is stabilized and trained to become familiar with the school's program, they can be given instructional responsibilities.

In the final analysis the teacher aide's position can only be justified in terms of the benefits it brings to children. Therefore, the only proper utilization of the aide is in a position in the classroom under the guidance of the teacher. Her primary concerns and actions within the classroom should be with the students and their educational and personal development. To use an aide to do nothing more than to duplicate materials or shuffle papers is to defeat the whole purpose of the position. The function of a teacher aide should differ only in degree and not in kind from that of the regular teacher.

THE TEACHER AIDE'S ROLE

Since the concept of teacher aides is relatively new, it is difficult to define terms clearly and concisely with the assurance that the terms will have the same meaning for everyone. In organizing a program, titles should be selected with care, roles should be defined, and functions should be specifically established. Role definition should establish the frame of reference; yet within these limitations role development should be flexible, adaptive, and dynamic. In this way changes can be made by utilizing an individual's special capabilities as she fits into a particular situation.

In the past little has been expected of aides beyond the handling of routine clerical chores. Quite often they were recruited from the ranks of housewives with only a high school diploma. Aides were expected to "pick up" the sundry skills and understandings considered essential for their job. Given this low expectation of the aide's role and the subsequent conclusion that they require only haphazard in-service preparation, their potential value as paraprofessionals has all too often been unrealized.

Adequately instructed aides can not only relieve the teacher from many mundane clerical and administrative tasks which presently hinder more creative and imaginative teaching, but also can themselves become involved in the instructional process. When aides are made sensitive to the nature of child growth and development they can play a significant role as a "second adult" with whom students can interact. Moreover, informed of the basic tenets of learning theory, aides can take an active part in actual instructional interaction with individual students, small groups, or even on occasion with the entire class. As aides are introduced to new instructional materials, equipment, techniques, and approaches to teaching basic concepts, they can serve as agents of change within the classroom.

Another important role teacher aides can perform within the educational structure is to serve as a liaison between the school and the community. For example, if the aide is a resident of the community from which the students come, she may often be asked to describe or even on occasion to defend school programs. It is imperative that information dispensed to the community be correct and properly presented. The teacher aide, additionally, can often provide staff members with important insights into community attitudes toward the school. It is important for you to be aware of this potential source of information and to utilize it on a continuing basis.

The value of an aide's assistance seems to be in direct relationship to her knowledge of the total school program. The teacher aide should be kept informed as to any innovations or adjustments within the program. An aide should also be kept informed of those daily activities that take place within the school, even though these may be occurring outside of her particular classroom. An informed aide can assist the teacher by providing an additional opinion or additional information which can be used by the teacher for program modification, alteration, or enrichment. In most cases this act of keeping the aide informed may be as simple as allowing her to read the daily school announcements. In some cases it may mean that the administration and the teacher will have to set aside meeting times to keep the aides informed as to program developments and modifications.

Nevertheless, the teacher who reaps the benefits of an aide has some adjustments to make, for she must change the operation of her classroom to include another adult. The teacher, too, must adjust to working in a new environment. There are some duties even she must learn to perform, not the least of which is the delineation of duties for her aide.

ASSIGNING TASKS

The duties that teacher aides are expected to perform encompass the gamut of the school's activities for the aide. Basically, the aide's services should be divided into roughly the three areas of clerical, instructional, and administrational. A day of balanced activities will provide the aide with a variety of experiences supportive of the educational program.

Regardless of the tasks you might choose to assign to your aide, you should provide her with a job description which outlines the functions of her position. If an aide does not know at least in a general way what is expected of her, she cannot function effectively.

The following pointers are intended to help you with the task of developing a job description for an aide:

- Begin by including those responsibilities that are easily described. These include such definite items as clerical, housekeeping, technical, and instructional tasks.
- Next consider the many activities that an aide can assist you with on an irregular basis. These might include developing special materials, working with student committees, accompanying a class on a field trip, etc.
- Finally, select from these activities some practices that can be agreed upon as describing effective aide behavior. These practices, plus the tasks listed above, should serve as the basis for an aide's tentative job description.

Many teachers have found it valuable to provide their aides with a brief but concise list of daily duties. While such a list would vary from classroom to classroom, the following suggestions might be a good starting point in developing your own job description for your teacher aide.

Routine Duties

1. Correct test papers that do not require subjective evaluation
2. Assist young children in putting on and taking off outdoor clothing
3. Aid teacher in an emergency situation if a child is hurt or ill
4. Assist with playground duties, hall duties, or bus chores under the direction of the teacher
5. Aid teacher in organizing recess time into directed games and activities
6. Help care for children in assembly programs

7. Assist in taking students to and from various places within the school (such as lunchroom, nurse's office, library, etc.)
8. Assist in taking a group of children on a field trip
9. Talk quietly with a student who is upset
10. Help students move from one activity to another
11. Help students learn to play together (such as sharing toys and materials, taking turns)
12. Read announcements to students
13. Complete routine forms
14. Perform clerical duties

Classroom Preparation

1. Operate equipment, such as movie projector, slide projector, tape recorder
2. Prepare audiovisual materials
3. Prepare bulletin board displays
4. File and catalog materials
5. Take attendance
6. Check supplies
7. Collect money
8. Get classroom ready for the next day
9. Check on temperature, fresh air, and lighting in the classroom

Instructional Duties

1. Play games with students, such as rhyming games, guessing games, finger games, etc.
2. Interest a restless student in some of the available activities
3. Listen to student talk such as in "show and tell"
4. Listen to a student tell a story
5. Listen to a student read
6. Assist a slow learner in finishing work or catching up
7. Act out stories with students
8. Read and tell stories to children
9. Take charge of a small group which is working on a teacher-assigned special project while the teacher works

with another group
10. Help students learn proper use of tools and equipment
11. Help students with instructional media
12. Help students to use programmed materials
13. Help students with subject matter missed during absences
14. Sing with a group of students
15. Play a musical instrument for students
16. Work directly with students in an art project which has been introduced, such as bulletin board, Christmas decorations, etc.
17. Help students get ready for an assembly program
18. Assist with teacher-assigned club activities
19. Help young children learn to use crayons, scissors, paste, paint
20. Distribute papers
21. Show students how to clear, organize, and put away materials
22. Help students locate information

DAILY PLANNING SCHEDULE

Teachers soon learn that the time aides spend in their rooms can be highly constructive if the teacher has planned worthwhile activities. This should not simply be a time for the aide to "sit in the back of the room" where she will become bored with the entire business of being in the classroom with children. Instead, you need to plan useful activities for her which will make her feel an important part of the instructional team.

The actual writing of plans and the amount of detail will depend greatly upon your own performance and experience with planning. Some teachers keep commercially prepared plan books covering all subject areas in brief outline form for each day; some teachers keep a running log; others devote a card or form for each daily curricular lesson.

Many teachers make the mistake of too much personal operation and too little constructive planning. If the teacher aide is going to do the job she was hired to do, then a great deal of planning will be required. Since planning requires looking ahead in terms of present and anticipated facts, it seems evident that planning requires analysis. Planning requires, then, a good deal of supervisory foresight.

Teaching an aide about planning must involve more than simply supplying her with a planning form. Instead, it demands that you work with her in such a way that she can write her own plans, utilize these plans, and also observe you as you develop and utilize your own plans. As you teach your aide to plan, you must strive to develop understanding, skills, and attitudes regarding the total process of effective planning for classroom teaching.

Providing your aide with a daily or even a weekly planning schedule will insure that she can make wise use of her time. Ideally, the aide should be involved in working out the schedule. In some cases she will be more aware of classroom needs than you will. In addition, if an aide serves more than one classroom she will be able to assist you in working out a schedule that does not conflict with her work elsewhere. Regardless of who is involved in the scheduling, you will find it productive to spend a few minutes each day in planning your aide's work.

It is suggested that you use a "daily planning schedule" similar to the format displayed in this section. To do this, you will need to have a supply of these forms duplicated. Space is provided on the form to specify the approximate time for each activity in which you will need your aide's assistance. A second column is provided to list or identify the teacher activity for which you will need help. Finally, the "aide's expected activities" are described in the appropriate column.

As your aide gains experience, you may find that her daily plans can become less detailed. When this point is reached, it may be possible to develop weekly or even long-range plans.

WEEKLY PLANNING

Your aide will not be able to rely upon daily plans alone. To only give her experience with a daily schedule is to "rob" her of

DAILY PLANNING SCHEDULE FOR AIDES

Teacher's Name		Aide's Name

Room No.		Date

Approximate Time	Teacher's General Plan	Aide's Expected Activities

a necessary experience in planning for longer blocks of time. You know very well that your own teaching demands that you plan for the week, the term, and even the year. Your teacher aide should get at least some experience with long-range planning. One effective way to provide experience in long-range planning is for you to plan each week with your aide.

It is not uncommon to find that teacher aides will have difficulty getting written plans to you when you want them. You may find that it is not always because she does not have them, however. Many times she may forget. Sometimes she is not sure of just when you want them or how to get them to you. The following suggestions may help you get the teacher aide's plans on time:

1. Provide the aide with a number of duplicated forms on which she can write her plans. This will also insure that the plans are uniform from week to week.

2. Make clear to your aide just when you want plans submitted. Giving this to her in writing may help insure that you get them on time.

3. Make a point to examine the plans in a manner that is obvious to the teacher aide. She will be encouraged to do a

better job and get the form in on time when she knows that you are taking the time to examine them.

4. Be consistent in your expectations regarding weekly plans. Remember that you do not make the aide's job easier when you permit sketchy or sloppily written plans.

Perhaps on Wednesday or Thursday you can begin to complete the planning sheet for the next week. It will be fairly easy for you to enter those subjects that you will teach and what you plan to do each day. The form can then be given to your aide on Friday morning, and she can complete her own planning sheet. You can then discuss the plan for the next week, and the aide can have a copy if she so desires. An alternative would be to post the aide's weekly planning form in the room each week so you, the teacher aide, and any observers can readily see what is being done and who is doing it. This weekly plan can then be used as specific daily lesson plans are developed throughout the week.

A sample "Weekly Planning Form" has been provided. You may desire to use this form or to develop a form that better meets your own particular needs. Regardless of your decision, you will find that the children in your room will benefit from the daily and weekly planning done by you and your aide.

AIDE'S WEEKLY PLANNING SCHEDULE					
Teacher's Name		Aide's Name		Date	
SUBJECT	MONDAY	TUESDAY	WEDNESDAY	THURSDAY	FRIDAY
Reading					
Social Studies					
Mathematics					
Lang. Arts					
Science					

Some classroom teachers report that they find it profitable to have aides keep a weekly log of activities they have participated in during the previous week. This procedure helps to insure continuity from week to week while providing the teacher with a written record of tasks aides have accomplished. In addition, the logs can be used to familiarize new aides with the kinds of duties they may expect. A typical "Weekly Log" has been prepared.

A SAMPLE TEACHER AIDE WEEKLY LOG

Monday

1. Adjusted ventilators
2. Mixed paints
3. Graded history test papers
4. Prepared notices to be sent home with children
5. Set up bookcase display
6. Made math flash cards
7. Helped child deal with personal problem
8. Hung posters and charts
9. Reviewed a book with children
10. Supervised boys on playground
11. Duplicated unit for math class
12. Corrected reading lab workbooks

Tuesday

1. Assisted in taking children to restrooms and encouraging good health habits
2. Discussed a geography filmstrip with children
3. Helped train children to march in and out
4. Worked out a key to correct a test in math
5. Rearranged bulletin board
6. Helped students with science unit
7. Worked with individual students in reading
8. Lined up students
9. Helped girl with her writing and instructed her in the use of a dictionary
10. Checked writing and spelling excercises
11. Supervised students taking science test
12. Supervised students in route to art class
13. Listened to children tell stories

Wednesday

1. Assisted with physical education
2. Helped children look up information
3. Secured needed reference books from the library
4. Aided in checking seat work
5. Assisted in supervising children on field trip
6. Aided in physical examinations
7. Helped children study for a test

8. Listened to children read individually
9. Took messages to the office

Thursday

1. Helped students review charts and graphs
2. Collected lunch money
3. Filed history and math papers
4. Prepared notices to be sent home with children
5. Typed test for teacher
6. Helped children clean up after art activity
7. Set up and operated overhead projector
8. Took children to cafeteria for lunch
9. Brought in nature study materials
10. Returned books to bookshelves
11. Aided in checking seat work
12. Helped with math drills
13. Worked with individual students
14. Supervised students taking reading test

Friday

1. Corrected (S.R.A.) reading laboratory books
2. Helped with gluing in art class
3. Helped students with math
4. Prepared and put away science equipment
5. Collected library fees
6. Made out requisition forms for teachers
7. Cleaned the chalkboard
8. Made transparencies for history class
9. Assisted in the supervision of classroom party
10. Distributed supplies to students
11. Gave make-up test in math
12. Supervised small group activities in science
13. Helped children look up science information
14. Helped supervise organized games
15. Secured materials from cabinets for class use

SUPERVISING INDIVIDUAL STUDENTS

One of the best entry tasks for aides in the area of instruction is that of assisting individual students with drill exercises, especially for remediation. Most elementary school classrooms have students in need of individualized remedial attention. Competent teacher aides, after some training, can be given the task of supervising areas where youngsters are working individually in spelling, reading, math, and science. The responsibilities that aides can assume in these situations include helping students to improve special skills, listening to oral reading, and repeating teacher-prepared instructions.

An obvious prerequisite for any aide to carry out instructional responsibilities is a thorough knowledge of what the children are to be taught. This information should be so deeply ingrained that it can easily be presented to youngsters. The aide should be familiar with the major instructional goals of the grade level or levels with which she works. In more detailed terms she must be acquainted with what is required of students in her assigned classroom. It is your responsibility to see that the aide is adequately prepared in regard to such matters.

Most educators agree that aides should not do initial instruction. That must remain the responsibility of the professional teacher. In the usual classroom, however, after the teacher has presented new instruction to the entire class, the students then either practice or meet in small groups to discuss the subject that has just been presented. The aide then can help children. The small group session will require someone to answer individual questions, to raise questions to which students should seek answers, and to explain matters that are not yet understood. If the initial instruction is followed by individual seatwork, the aide can quickly find students who need help, thus preventing them from becoming frustrated or discouraged.

Of course, the aide is not expected to have remedial teaching skills or be an expert in subject matter. For example, she cannot be expected to teach reading the way a highly professional teacher does. Nevertheless, her job is to work toward helping the youngsters to become successful readers. An aide can assist you by encouraging a child to read, by giving the child her full attention when he is reading, by letting him know that she enjoys reading, by helping him to group the words into meaningful phrases, and by always being patient. Aides are most successful when they use encouragement freely, look for something to praise, and are not sarcastic.

To illustrate how an aide can assist with instruction, we will use the case of a reading teacher who has been working with her class of third graders and who has already diagnosed the wide variances in the ability of the youngsters. While the aide supervises the rest of the class as they work independently on suffixes, the teacher can select a small group of students for diagnostic purposes. She may discover that the five slowest students in the classroom cannot function because they are still unable to recognize syllables in words. When she has diagnosed a common deficiency in the group, she can call the aide to the group and give her specific instructions about remedial activities to perform with the entire group.

At this point the aide can reinforce what the classroom teacher has already begun with the students. With the reading class it may be a simple matter of giving children further practice in counting syllables and using words that have been divided into syllables. The aide can work closely with the students in a natural teaching situation, asking questions about correct pronunciation or answering questions about a step in the process.

Another example would be a math teacher who has been working in some phase of general mathematics with fifth grade students. After identifying students who need help, she can then turn the group over to the aide for drill work. The aide, with specific instructions, can assist the youngsters in reviewing, for example, their multiplication tables.

While working with students, your aide may discover that a student needs specific instructions from you, in which case she could wait for an opportunity to relieve you so that you might come to the group for reinforcement or reteaching. After helping the student, you may then return the group to the aide who continues with the assistance upon which you have decided.

However, with a slower-paced class there will usually be more one-to-one instruction such as listening to lessons, going over math problems, reviewing, and drill work. The aide in a faster-paced classroom may spend more time working with students, locating supplemental instructional materials, setting up science equipment, or supervising the use of materials. The teacher aide will have different responsibilities, depending on the type of self-contained classroom or supportive service (remedial reading, library, etc.) to which she is assigned.

Just remember, when working with your aide you must rely upon your own professional judgment when assigning any kind of instructional duties. The kind and quantity of work she will be able to do will depend on the competency of the aide and must be left to your discretion. Each classroom teacher must find various ways to use her aide — increasing the aide's duties as experience and teacher judgment command.

SMALL GROUP INSTRUCTION

Most teachers find it difficult, if not impossible to teach basic skills in large groups. The range of skills existing in a single classroom is so extreme as to make this task difficult for any teacher. On the other hand, teaching skills to children on a one-to-one basis can be a waste of an instructor's valuable and limited time. The small group affords an opportunity to instruct students in an economical and efficient manner. A child is given enough attention to build a particular skill while at the same time he is not being overwhelmed by individual attention.

When a second person, in this case a teacher aide, is introduced into the classroom, little excuse remains to use traditional class size as the basic instructional unit. A small group organization permits the teacher or aide to hear a limited number of students quickly and note their errors for correction. In addition, the small group maintains high student interest levels since there is a rich, though not overwhelming, amount of student-teacher interaction.

Determining the size of a small group with which an aide can effectively work will depend on both the ability and experience of the teacher aide. Since open communication between the students and the aide is important, probably four to six students should be considered the maximum number that an aide should work with at one time. Some groups might be increased to eight or ten members and still function effectively, as when the aide is reading a story. When, however, interaction between the student and instructor is required, any group larger than six would not be appropriate.

Assigning students to a small group is a decision you must make. Many times that can be done in consultation with your aide. The students can be grouped by interest, ability, or personality. More often than not the nature of the group activity will determine its composition as well as the number of students included.

Typically in the elementary school classroom the small group concept is utilized in reading instruction. The teacher will divide the class into from three to five reading groups depending on the range of ability students exhibit and on the aide's ability to handle one or more of the groups. Dividing the reading class into small groups helps the teacher to assess the progress of individuals through question-and-answer sessions and group discussion. In addition, working with small groups gives the teacher an opportunity to introduce new reading skills and word-attack procedures while the aide is reinforcing or reviewing previous instruction.

The role you assign to a teacher aide in this type of instruction will vary depending on your primary objective. An aide might be expected to listen to recitations, conduct a discussion, drill children on a particular skill, clarify a concept, or review for a test. The aide should be expected to keep accurate records, to seek your advice on the steps to follow, and to report to you the progress and achievement of the students.

Whenever you elect to conduct small group work in cooperation with your teacher aide, she can perform the following services in handling the students:

1. Helping the students to organize their equipment, supplies, or information
2. Supervising students to make certain they are following your directions
3. Tutoring and reviewing remedial groups
4. Administering simple quizzes to students in accordance with your instructions
5. Operating audiovisual equipment for the group while they work

AIDES WITH SPECIAL TALENTS

In any examination of the duties to be assigned aides, some mention should be made of aides with special skills. For example, an aide with musical talent might teach children songs, help them develop their sense of rhythm, or even teach them to play the piano. An aide who is an artist can help youngsters explore line, color, form, and texture. An individual with a background in the theater might provide experience in drama for a group of interested students.

Every community has people with talent, people with unusual hobbies, and people with special knowledge. When employed as teacher aides, these individuals are able to provide children with stimulation and experience they would not otherwise have in their regular school program. The kind of relationship which can be built up between a young child and an aide can sometimes be critical to his development. An aide can give undivided attention to a child for a long period of time, can listen to his words, and become sensitive to his unvoiced wishes.

The modern classroom offers numerous opportunities for teacher aides to be creative. For example, ask your aide if she would enjoy reading stories to children, writing stories, or enjoy telling them. Does your aide sew or crochet? Maybe your aide or one in a nearby room has made costumes for a play or painted scenery. Perhaps your aide is mechanically inclined. Such people are needed to run motion picture projectors and set up tape recorders and other audiovisual equipment. If your aide speaks a foreign language or has traveled widely and collected slides or other souvenirs youngsters might enjoy, you can use her experience effectively in your classroom.

Any willing individual can be trained to contribute a great deal to your classroom. However, give your new teacher aide an opportunity to share her varied talents with the students in your room. More than one classroom teacher has discovered late in the school year that her aide has some undiscovered talent which, if uncovered earlier, would have contributed immeasurably to the education of children in her class. Some teachers have found it useful to ask each new aide to complete an "interest inventory" in order to become acquainted with any special talents early in the school year. An example of a typical interest inventory is presented in this section. Why not use it with your teacher aide?

TEACHER AIDE INTEREST INVENTORY

Name_____   Date_____

Address_____   Phone_____

Status (full - or part-time)_____

Education (high school, college, etc.)_____

_____

1. What (if any) are your career goals?
   a. Present:_____

   b. Future:_____

2. Why were you interested in becoming a teacher aide?_____

_____

3. List your experiences with children (Sunday school, baby sitting, etc.)

_____

4. What other work experience have you had?_____

_____

5. Have you ever done supervisory work? If yes, explain._____

6. What were your favorite subjects in school?_____

7. What hobbies or interests do you have?_____

8. What special skills or talents do you have which will help you in your teacher aide
   work?_____

9. What age group or grade level appeals to you the most?
   _____ Pre-school (ages 2-5)
   _____ Kindergarten - 3rd Grade (ages 5-8)
   _____ Intermediate - 4th Grade - 6th Grade (ages 9-12)

10. What questions or problems do you have regarding work as a teacher aide?

_____

_____

ASSISTING WITH LARGE GROUPS

Teacher aides can be of invaluable assistance with large group instruction. They are especially helpful in supervising study areas within the elementary school. Aides can also assist teachers in supervising large groups of students in cafeterias, gymnasiums, and study halls. Many teachers use aides to escort groups to and from special classes, rest rooms, the cafeteria, and assembly programs. Likewise, aides can monitor tests and can be responsible for distributing and collecting test booklets and answer sheets.

Large group instruction can be both an economical and efficient way of teaching. This method can be used for lecturing, giving directions, making assignments, administering tests, and conducting projects. Bringing the entire class together for certain activities strengthens the feeling of belonging for a large group, and it can help establish a sense of community. The entire class learns to live together by sharing experiences, setting up rules and regulations, and by exchanging ideas and opinions.

If you choose to use your aide in large group instruction, it will be a good idea to clearly define her role. Seldom, if ever, should she be responsible for teaching the entire class. However, you might elect to ask her to show a film or filmstrip to the large group or to administer a group test, either standardized or teacher-made. On occasion you may want to let the aide check an assignment with the entire group or to explain the homework papers that you have already graded.

It is of utmost importance to the overall functioning of your aide when assisting large group instruction that the teacher aide thoroughly understand the philosophical and organizational aspects of your program. Well-defined guidelines within which the aide can function are also necessary. Exactly what is the aide expected to do? How is she to accomplish the task? And, how much discretion will she be allowed in carrying out her assignment?

DUTIES OF THE TEACHER AIDE

No two teacher aides experience identical duties. Assignments vary according to the needs of the school and the discretion of the teacher. Teacher aides may perform any of the following duties. The nature of the duties will naturally vary according to the grade level of students and the type of classroom.

I. Noninstructional Functions

A. Community-related functions
1. Collect money for charity drives, pupil pictures, and other causes
2. Telephone parents about routine matters at the request of the teacher
3. Make arrangements for field trips, collect parental permission forms and other forms

B. Curriculum
1. Collect and display pictures, objects, and models
2. Collect supplementary books and materials for instruction
3. Compile bibliographies for particular areas of study
4. Correct standardized and informal tests and prepare student profiles and scattergrams under the supervision of the teacher
5. Correct homework and workbooks, noting and reporting weak areas
6. Proofread class newspaper
7. Keep records on books children have read

C. Physical Facilities
1. Order and return films, filmstrips, and other audiovisual materials
2. Distribute books and supplies to students
3. Distribute and collect specific materials for lessons, such as writing paper, art paper, and supplies
4. Procure, set up, operate, and return instructional equip-

ment
5. Supervise clean-up time
6. Requisition supplies under the direction of the teacher
7. Build up resource collection
8. Obtain special materials for science and other projects
9. Account for and inventory nonconsumable classroom books, athletic gear, and other equipment

D. Daily School Program
1. Collect lunch and/or milk money
2. Send for free and inexpensive materials with the approval of the teacher
3. Complete necessary records and bring other information up to date in cumulative folders
4. Post grades on report cards
5. Enter grades in the marking book of the teacher
6. Attend to housekeeping chores
7. Help with clothing of the children
8. Telephone parents of absent children
9. Telephone parents to verify notes requesting that children leave school early
10. Take attendance reports and classify them
11. Run errands; handle routine interruptions such as messages, deliveries, and visitors

E. Instruction-related Functions
1. Supervise the classroom in case of emergencies
2. Assist the teacher in the supervision of the playground, cafeteria, and bus loading, gym and locker rooms, halls, and rest rooms
3. Arrange and supervise indoor games on rainy days
4. Prepare and supervise work areas, such as arranging materials for accessibility, putting down drop cloths, mixing paint, and similar details
5. Organize and supervise the intramural programs under the supervision of the professional staff
6. Check out books in the central library
7. Manage room libraries
8. Supervise student seatwork
9. Type the correspondence of the teacher to parents

10. Type and duplicate instructional materials
11. Type and duplicate the class newspaper
12. Type and duplicate the writings and other work of the children
13. Keep a folder of representative work for each child
14. Display student work
15. Attend to the weighing, measuring, and eye testing of students
16. Prepare stencils and masters, transparencies, overlays, charts, posters, maps, and other visual aids
17. Operate the mimeograph and Ditto® machines

II. Semiinstructional Functions

A. Community-Related Functions
   1. Supervise school club meetings under the supervision of the teacher
   2. Supervise committees engaged in painting murals, constructing, researching, or experimenting, under the supervision of the teacher
   3. Teach good manners
   4. Assist with field trips
B. Curriculum
   1. Conduct story hour by reading and telling stories
   2. Interest a restless student in some of the available activities
   3. Help students look up information in a resource book
C. Physical Facilities
   1. Prepare instructional materials
   2. Arrange bulletin board displays for teaching purposes such as flow charts
   3. Keep bulletin boards current
   4. Arrange interesting and inviting corners for learning
   5. Prepare introductions to audiovisual materials that give children the background for viewing them
   6. Assist children in the proper use and safety of tools and equipment
   7. Preview films and other audiovisual materials

8. Classify and organize instructional materials
9. Help with arrangements — help move desks and chairs; supervise students in eraser dusting and board cleaning; help with interest centers, adjust ventilation and lighting to keep them healthful

D. Daily School Program
  1. Assist students in interpreting directions
  2. Encourage completion of work
  3. Supervise independent student study and work
  4. Help students to settle arguments without fighting
  5. Talk quietly to a student who is upset
  6. Help children to improve special skills
  7. Talk with children who have specific problems, upon the request of the teacher
  8. Drill a part of the class in a simple understanding, skill, or appreciation
  9. Drill a small and temporary instructional group in the mechanics of reading, writing, and speaking
  10. Tutor individual children
  11. Review or summarize learning for children
  12. Review with children who missed instruction because they were out of the room for illness
  13. Help students with their compositions and other writings
  14. Listen to oral reading by students
  15. Prepare materials for home-bound students and assist students with make-up work
  16. Assist substitute teachers in planning work
  17. Help to reinforce skills in small groups or with individual students
  18. Monitor discussions in small groups
  19. Place written work on chalkboard

E. Other Duties
  1. Help with fire drills
  2. Supervise activities such as those found in programmed materials
  3. Repair materials and books
  4. Assist in the supervision of children in the library

SUMMARY

The assignment of specific teacher aide duties should be preceded by an assessment of a particular school's needs. This assessment should consider the instructional priorities of the school, with the primary goal always being improved student learning. In a period when the operation of schools has become diversified and complex, priorities will of course vary from classroom to classroom. In all cases, however, the assistance which aides might provide is limited only by the creativity and initiative of the school staff.

Some schools, for example, may determine that aides can release teachers from many clerical and housekeeping tasks. Releasing teachers and other school personnel from these chores will enable them to concentrate their efforts upon instructional functions. Other schools may elect to utilize aides in the preparation and operation of educational media. Still other schools may be able to employ aides as instructional members of the teaching team.

The function and role of the aide should be precisely defined, yet innovations should be possible as new needs emerge and as an aide demonstrates on-the-job growth. As an aide works in a particular classroom with its rules and regulations, its space and equipment, the teacher should constantly evaluate what the aide does and decide what changes should be made as they move toward their established educational goals.

CHAPTER 4

INDIVIDUALIZING INSTRUCTION

I NDIVIDUALIZED instruction is well on the way to becoming an accepted procedure in elementary school classrooms across the nation. Few arguments can be found against the merits of classrooms moving in the direction of individualizing instruction for students. With the advent of accountability programs, performance testing, etc. the need for teaching on the instructional level of each child is becoming a pressing issue. Ideally, individualized instruction permits the gifted student to move as rapidly as possible while the slow learner is helped by means of tutoring and frequent reinforcement.

In providing for individual differences within your classroom, you must recognize the unique differences among the students and the varying needs of the children assigned to you. An effective program must be organized with appropriate instructional patterns and materials to meet these needs and to match the student's different responses to appropriate teaching methods or techniques. A child learns more effectively when he is presented with learning opportunities in the form of materials and tasks for which he is ready. Learning is enhanced when each student is rewarded for his correct responses and when he meets the teacher's expectations for him.

Individual contact with children can also give you a much deeper insight into the educational needs of a student. In what areas of instruction does he seem to be deficient? In what subject areas does he possess superior insight? What does he like or dislike? To be in possession of such information is to have access to the keys of learning for individual students. For example, to find that a student loves music is to find a new way to reinforce his reading and communication skills. Another who enjoys sports can be assisted through this vehicle to read, write, and speak more effectively.

The teacher aide can play an important role in all efforts to individualize instruction. You would find it almost impossible to work effectively with an individual student if you had no assistance with the remainder of the class. An aide can be of assistance to you in at least two broadly defined categories. First, she can free you from many of the time-consuming tasks such as grading papers, recording attendance, and taking the lunch count, thus freeing you to concentrate on endeavors which contribute to individualizing. Secondly, if properly trained, your aide can actually work with groups of students or individuals under your direction and supervision.

RATIONALE FOR INDIVIDUALIZATION

One basic belief that is central to the concept of individualized instruction is the belief that distinct individual differences exist among any group of students for whom we are accountable. It is appalling to consider the misguided efforts that are expended in the search for one "cure-all" instructional program which will serve the needs of all students. Anyone who truly accepts the tenet of the existence of individual differences and who sees the necessity of assisting students to meet their individual needs would have to support the application of individualization techniques in teaching-learning situations. Therefore, there must be potentially as many ways or programs for learning as there are students — such is the process of individualization.

Many educators believe that the traditional approach to instruction is unacceptable because it is not responsive enough to modern instructional needs. For instance, it does not encourage initiative on the part of the individual learner, nor does it give him credit for exploratory or innovative learning activities. Although some teachers are slow to realize and accept this idea, students must be encouraged to appraise their own strengths and weaknesses and to learn how to devise their own instructional activities.

When elementary teachers are first introduced to individualized instruction, they often envision a system of total chaos.

They have difficulty perceiving children as being capable of making the many decisions necessary to maintain an orderly classroom. When chaos does occur in an individualized program, it is usually because teachers have not permitted students to be sufficiently involved in the decision-making process; and very likely they have not encouraged them to accept responsibility for their own growth in the past. Such training will require the cooperative effort of teachers, aides, and students. In this, as in other educational undertakings, each student must operate as an individual who needs to develop skills at a rate appropriate for achieving synthesis with the skills he has already acquired.

If you want to develop an individualized program you should be aware of the change of emphasis in the role you will have in the classroom. First, you must serve as a kind of curriculum counselor in the area of instruction. In an individualized program the appropriateness of the curriculum is not determined for the entire class as a group but, instead, must be determined for each student on the basis of his needs, abilities, and interests. The counseling process is a continual reassessment of the above criteria, and the resulting decision should be a cooperative effort by you and the student. Instructional counseling should involve the diagnosis of a child's progress and the reinforcement of his achievement. Secondly, in an individualized program you must assume the task, to some degree, of modifying behavior. As you become more aware of individual student behavior, you must plan procedures for helping each student to modify his behavior by using techniques that you have planned on the basis of the individual student's characteristics.

HOW TO ACHIEVE INDIVIDUALIZATION

It is one thing to speak of individualized instruction and quite another to actually accomplish it within an elementary classroom. If twenty educators were to be asked for their definition of individualization, probably twenty different answers would be forthcoming. Possibly, this is simply an indication that the concept of individualization is still in its formative stages. Because of the variety of definitions, however, it is essential that the meaning of individualization as it relates to the elementary school classroom be fully understood by teachers.

The term individualizing refers to any approach to instruction which serves to meet the instructional needs of students and which recognizes that the traditional group approach is inadequate. Individualization also means personalization of instruction to meet the needs of each student; it does not mean a single program designed to meet the needs of all.

Possibly the first, and apparently the most popular, definition of individualization defines it in terms of the time element. Obviously, no two individuals need to cover the same material at the same rate on exactly the same day. Instead of lecturing to the entire class and covering the subject matter in sequential order, you can work individually with each student. However, for the student, individualization with respect to time means little more than that it is acceptable to differ in the rate of learning from one's fellow students.

Once the pervasive practice of having students attempt to work at the same rate at the same time was overcome, it was only natural to question the concept of "same material." Is it necessary that all students cover the same basic content? Answers, of course, range from a very conservative view that all students must master an essential curriculum to the other extreme view that it is necessary to have a totally unstructured curriculum with little, if any, required content. Since a middle-of-the-road approach is usually closer to reality, it is often appropriate to operate under the assumption that certain basic skills form the essential groundwork for any study, including elementary school studies. Various optional or alternate topics for study then may be prescribed to satisfy individual needs and interests.

A final definition of individualization concerns the instructional approach used by each individual to reach his learning goals. In this regard numerous research studies have agreed on two basic conclusions: (1) different individuals learn best by using different instructional approaches, and (2) a combination of instructional approaches is better than any one alone. An attempt should be make to identify the approach most effective for each individual, and then his or her learning program should be built around this approach.

Teachers who plan to initiate individualized instruction should be aware that implementation of the program will necessitate a need for a greater variety of instructional materials. Even for the individual who likes to learn by reading, it will be necessary not to rely solely on this form of instruction so that the student will not lose interest. The primary concern must be for a wider variety of instructional materials that are acceptable to the student and that will be actively used by him.

To truly individualize instruction within the classroom a systematic and sequential organizational scheme is required which will arrange subject matter content from the least complicated skills to the most challenging. Therefore, regardless of his grade level a student could be placed at his own instructional level and advanced from that point as he masters each sequential level. Inherent within this organizational plan is the idea that the less academically able student may take more time in mastering the content while the academically superior student may be constantly challenged by new material.

Also inherent within individualized programs is the idea that a student will complete one set of work acceptably before moving on the next level. This requires that a close scrutiny be made of the progress of each student. Assistance and direction must be given when needed; testing must be used at the appropriate time; and materials for the student's next learning experience must be ready for immediate use. In addition, some type of daily record-keeping system which reflects an academic profile of each individual student must be developed.

PERFORMANCE OBJECTIVES

It is imperative that performance objectives be formulated as a first step in individualizing instruction. While it is assumed that most teachers are familiar with both the rationale and mechanics of utilizing performance objectives, a brief review of the rudiments of the subject might prove beneficial. Basically, performance objectives are statements which describe what a student will be expected to accomplish upon completing a prescribed unit of instruction or a series of activities. Similarly, objectives describe the final outcome of instruction in terms of observable behavior, stating the conditions under which the final performance will be judged. This type of objective informs the learner what behavior he is expected to achieve. In contrast, nonbehaviorally stated objectives usually lack specificity and usually do not indicate how the learner is to demonstrate what he has learned.

Objectives help to insure that instructional activities are result oriented. Planning based upon well-defined objectives compels a continuous renewal process to be set in motion. Unless performance objectives are utilized, teachers will have little basis upon which to measure the effectiveness of the individual components of the instructional program. In the past too much stress has been placed upon informal methods of evaluating the effectiveness of instruction.

The function of performance objectives as a prerequisite for planning and evaluating individualized instruction can best be shown by presenting the basic elements essential to a well-written objective—

1. *Behavior:* A description of expected terminal behavior which can be observed by at least two independent observers
2. *Conditions:* A statement of the conditions under which the behavior is to be observed
3. *Criteria:* A statement of the criteria of acceptable performance including the means or instrument which will be used to measure performance

Above all else a well-defined and forcefully stated objective must succeed in communicating an instructional intent. Whenever possible individualized objectives should be written in quantitative language, requiring results that are stated in definite, measurable terms. Although learning is usually internalized as ideas or concepts, there are always outward manifestations of that which is learned. Behavior outcomes usually offer the best clues to what has been learned from an instructional experience. Accordingly, for each objective you should select those specific behavioral outcomes which are most likely to reflect progress toward achieving a goal.

In attempting to specify performance objectives in an individualized program, it is advisable to use verbs which denote action. Verb forms that involve doing should be used to identify the overall act or behavior. Obviously verb forms such as *to write, to identify, to reconstruct, to itemize,* and *to calculate* are more explicit indicators of behavior than are *to know, to appreciate,* and *to believe.* Thus, *to identify* the basic components of a well-written objective is easier to observe and evaluate than is *to understand* the components of a well-written objective.

Although it is apparent that both practice and experience play an important role in developing one's skill in writing well-defined performance objectives, some suggestions might prove beneficial to the neophyte. These include the following:

1. State each objective in terms of the participant's performance rather than of the teacher's performance.
2. State each objective as a learning product rather than as a learning process.
3. State each objective so it will indicate terminal behavior rather than the content to be covered during the instructional process.
4. State each objective so it will include only one learning outcome rather than a combination of outcomes.
5. State each objective so that each specific learning outcome will start with a verb that indicates observable behavior.

TUTORING

In an individualized classroom, tutoring is the most commonly used instructional technique. Tutoring usually takes precedence over large group instruction for two basic reasons. First, children are working on a variety of objectives; therefore, it is ineffective to give an explanation of a concept either before or after a student needs it. Secondly, students usually vary in their need for assistance.

Tutoring includes these three basic steps:

1. *Diagnosing the problem* — Encourage the student to take the initiative in discovering his own educational weaknesses. Ask him what he thinks the problem is. Question him about the relevant skills or concepts in which he is proficient. Check his proficiency in all the relevant skills or concepts.

2. *Demonstrating the skill or concept* — After the difficulty has been identified by you or the student, demonstrate the use of the skill or discuss the concept. Always use concrete materials or put the concept into a context with which the student is familiar. Too often, teachers assume that a context that is familiar to them is also familiar to the child. A sketch, a picture, an anecdote, or a description that the student can relate to is always helpful. Most teachers have found that they interact with their students so frequently when using individualized instruction that they therefore know their students better and can relate to the students' experiences much more effectively.

3. *Student demonstration of proficiency* — The third step is to have the student demonstrate his proficiency in the skill or concept. To simply ask a student, "Do you understand?" and rely on a positive response does not give sufficient evidence of his proficiency. Rather, the student must demonstrate his skill or use the new concept. It is for this reason that most teachers in individualized classrooms have found that tutoring a single child is much more effective than trying to teach a large group. Each student can then demonstrate his proficiency. As he does so, he can start working independently more often so the teacher's time can be more efficiently spent with a student who is having trouble.

Remember, when tutoring a student, do not force learning. Sometimes a child will have more important things to do than schoolwork. An occasional session with the student will be much more profitable in the long run and will contribute to a more productive instructional relationship. Forcing a student to perform an educational task when he is highly resistent to it will reduce his interest for the subject while at the same time hurt your relationship with him. Persistence, patience, and kindness are the best means of cutting through a student's resistance to schoolwork.

In working with students, most teachers have found that the better their personal relationship is with the student and the greater the student's trust is in the teacher, the easier it is for the teacher to use this relationship to lead the student into learning areas he would never attempt on his own. You can become much more deeply involved with a student when he sees your demands as an attempt to assist him instead of as an act of punishment. As the student progresses further in the tutoring relationship, the level of assistance can be gradually reduced.

INDIVIDUALLY PRESCRIBED INSTRUCTION

The goal of individually prescribed instruction is to provide each student with a variety of instructional materials and approaches to meet his individual needs. Individually prescribed instructional materials are carefully sequenced according to detailed behavioral objectives.

Within this program each student has a thorough diagnosis made by means of a diagnostic pretest to determine what he has mastered in a specific curriculum area and what he still needs to learn. The child is then expected to proceed through prepared materials relevant to instructional objectives as determined by the pretests. Of course, students are expected to work at a rate appropriate for them rather than to keep pace with the entire class. No student need slow or speed his rate of learning merely to accommodate other children in the classroom. The child who is a fast learner may be challenged by moving as rapidly as his development dictates. The opposite is also true — the slow learner may avoid undue frustration by not being pushed beyond his learning capacity.

Once the pretesting is completed, you determine the starting point for each child in your room. On the basis of this diagnosis a prescription is developed for each student. This prescription lists the materials which the child should use to begin his study. At this point the student will begin working independently on the prescribed materials. Most students will be able to proceed through the materials with a minimum amount of teacher or aide direction or assistance. As soon as the child is working independently or with a teacher aide, you are free for instructional decision making, evaluation of student progress, and scoring tests and worksheets.

Probably one of the primary reasons for the failure of individually prescribed instruction is the teacher's inability to keep adequate materials prepared for each student. Instructional materials should be selected with the needs of each child in mind. If these materials are to have meaning for students, the selection must be based on knowledge of individual abilities, achievement, and interest. In addition, teachers must have available the results of periodic achievement tests, teacher-made diagnostic tests, and student interest inventories.

Most teachers construct learning packets to fit the particular requirements for children in their classroom. However, commercially developed learning packets are available for teachers who do not have the time or resources to produce their own. Learning packets are instructional modules that contain one or more instructional objectives. Usually the packet or package contains a pretest, sample test items, a bibliography of study references, and a list of instructional materials that are available to help the student accomplish the behavioral objective.

The well-trained teacher aide can be invaluable in collecting or helping to prepare the appropriate books, worksheets, learning packets, etc., necessary to keep students working at their maximum pace. Directly related to the dispensing of student materials is the collection and checking of these materials. The sheer volume of paper work, record keeping, and evaluation feedback to the student is staggering and beyond the reach of most teachers who are trying to individualize without any assistance. The aide's assistance can help make individualization a reality.

INTEREST CENTERS

The importance of learner self-direction in individualized instruction has long been recognized. The term *learning center,* or *interest center,* more nearly describes areas of the classroom in which the teacher has established a place in which interests are developed and problems may be more fully explored. Depending upon both the maturity and the interests of students, different learning centers may be developed within your classroom. Centers could be designed to meet individual student interests in a variety of subject areas, such as arithmetic centers, science corners, reading centers, etc.

Most teachers find that elaborate materials and a great deal of space are not required to develop interest centers in their classrooms. For instance, a table, some chairs, and a bookcase could be utilized to make an interest center. Cardboard boxes can be remodeled and turned into satisfactory work tables and bookcases. Often children can bring various materials, books, games, puzzles, and magazines from home.

In developing a center, the instructional needs of the slow learner, as well as those of superior students, must be kept in mind. Materials should be selected by both the teacher and the aide. Assistance should be available at all times, and this should include help with non-book materials as well as printed materials. However, as in all individualized undertakings, the students' use of the interest center is the final measure of its success. Not only should students be permitted to use the centers, they must have time in their daily schedule to go there. Rules governing movement to and from the interest center must be as nonrestrictive as possible. Children have to be taught what the interest centers are for and how to use them. This responsibility belongs to the teacher and her aide and may have to be repeated several times. It will be helpful if, as centers are developed, you can print guidelines on a large chart to be kept visible for those who need reminders.

During learning center activities, teacher aides can be used not only for doing the housekeeping chores and putting centers together, but they can also be used to act as feedback agents.

Aides, as feedback agents, can be expected to interact with a child in a general manner such as:

1. reading directions to students
2. assisting children in spelling words
3. monitoring
4. having a key to correct written exercises
5. typing creative stories dictated by students

INDEPENDENT STUDY

The classroom teacher faces a challenge in meeting the needs of students with marked differences in abilities. Encouraging independent study by the student helps you to meet this challenge by providing a wide selection of student activities. The use of this approach permits different rates of progress by students while giving them an opportunity to reach in all directions for educational goals and experiences.

Teachers need to provide individual students with opportunities to study and work apart from the entire group. Not only do pupils need to develop responsibility for their own learning, according to their own interests and abilities, but they also need to encounter challenges that bring forth intellectual inquiry and creativity. Group assignments that result in conventional homework deny students the best opportunities for independent study and investigation.

To be effective, however, independent study must be a part of, not apart from, the regular instructional program. Its emphasis must be on creative, meaningful assignments that strengthen a student's research skills. Properly conducted, it will help pupils grow in self-correction, self-analysis, and self-direction.

In addition, teachers and aides have a particular responsibility to help students learn how to study. Many students require a more independent approach to studying. Most teachers find that even well-motivated students need to improve their techniques of studying. However, large quantities of inappropriate homework assignments do not facilitate good study habits, but instead actually promote bad habits.

One of the primary results of independent study is that the teacher becomes dispensable rather than indispensable. For example, after the completion of an independent study unit, the student merely reports to the instructional aide for a copy of the examination. He completes the test, returns to the aide, and immediately proceeds to the next concept to be learned. The test paper is graded by the aide with limited assistance from the teacher.

However, in utilizing your aide in independent study, keep in mind that she must know the subject matter well enough to answer questions or to refer a student to you when special assistance is required. Such an arrangement not only saves you time, but also removes a temptation on your part to oversupervise students.

During independent study an aide can assume responsibilities such as the following:

1. Circulating in the classroom to see if children are completing their work
2. Working on a specific skill with individual students
3. Providing emotional support and close supervision for the child having behavioral problems
4. Giving or repeating teacher-prepared instructions
5. Assisting students in looking up information

THE ROLE OF THE AIDE

Self-teaching is a term often used to describe individualized instruction. If this is truly the case, what is the role of the teacher aide? The first step is directing the use of the materials themselves. There are individualized materials for beginning skills through upper-level skills. In the beginning stage of learning, the children will need a great deal of teacher and aide guidance before they will be able to work independently through the materials. Later, the children will be able to work with only a minimum of assistance.

The properly trained teacher aide can be effectively utilized to perform most of the routine tasks germane to individualized instruction. When she is properly utilized, the pitfalls of this type of instruction can be minimal. Records can be kept complete and up-to-date, children can be kept functioning at their optimum level, a high degree of personal contact can be maintained with each student, the volume of necessary clerical work can be more adequately handled, and the teacher can apply her talents more directly to those individuals who are more in need of her assistance.

For instance, the aide can easily do a daily check upon the progress of each student, identifying and providing materials needed, clarifying questions or problems, administering evaluation techniques when needed, and maintaining the record-keeping system. Referrals of specific students can then be made to you for actual reteaching or academic assistance requiring the attention of a professionally trained individual. Thus the aide, under your direction, can keep direct contact with each child so that individual progress is maintained and nurtured on a daily basis.

Although diagnosing and prescribing are the responsibilities of the teacher, the follow-up and implementation of the academic program are very much within the grasp of most properly trained teacher aides. The aide can prove invaluable in assisting children in completing assignments and doing drill work on, for example, basic mathematics or reading skills. If an aide has the skill to resolve a particular reading problem and the teacher can more profitably be occupied with another child, then this should be the plan. Individual instruction should never be the exclusive territory of either you or the aide; rather, it should depend on the individual skills of each one.

During individualized instruction aides might be utilized to do the following:

1. Keep records
2. Pass out and collect student materials
3. Work with students as they use programmed materials
4. Assist students in understanding directions (oral or written)
5. Read material that students find too difficult
6. Play educational games with students
7. Assist in moving students from one activity to another

8. Visit the library to help students select books
9. Gather information about work habits of students
10. Use audiovisual equipment with students
11. Develop a bulletin board display with students.

SUMMARY

While the teacher aide must retain her singular identity, she must also be capable of amalgamation with the instructional team. As we attempt to move closer to providing both realistic and actual individualized instruction, there must be a teacher aide to assist the professional teacher and to help assure the successful implementation of individualized instructional programs. There can be little doubt that an aide's assistance will be a major factor in how successfully individualized instruction is carried out.

Regardless of the context, individualized instruction is at best a very time-consuming, arduous task. Satisfactory accomplishment of the learning task is usually out of the reach of most individual classroom teachers. Therefore, the properly recruited and trained teacher aide offers the valuable potential needed for the ultimate success of the classroom seriously trying to program for and cope with individual learning differences.

Skill in individualized study can be attained only through practice on assignments of increasing difficulty. As the student's success increases, his ability to learn independently and his willingness to assume some responsibility for his own learning increase in direct proportion. Providing the needed successful experience is a joint responsibility of the teacher and the teacher aide.

CHAPTER 5

READING INSTRUCTION

F EW people would doubt the importance that reading claims in the area of classroom achievement or its importance for success later in life. Reading plays an indispensable role in our lives. Frequently it is considered the single most important subject in the elementary school curriculum. Many parents consider reading the only important subject taught in our schools. Testing in all subjects often measures no more than a child's ability to read the test items. For these reasons reading instruction is one area in which the classroom aide should be well versed.

It would be well for all of us to remember that in teaching reading almost every student within the normal range of intelligence can be taught to read. It cannot be emphasized enough that motivation, exposure, and consistent practice are the best means of insuring reading success. The greatest deficiency present in most reading programs is the lack of effective practice. Since unused skills are of little value, we must instill in children a love for reading.

One of the best ways to make learning to read interesting and exciting is to help children understand what reading is and what the process can mean in their daily lives. Have you asked children to define reading? Have you had them consider what they read and how it is of value to them? Have you caused them to wonder why reading and writing were created long ago and why these processes endure?

Surveys have indicated that more teachers utilize aides in reading instruction than in any other academic area within the curriculum. However, teachers often have not adequately oriented or trained aides to assist them in teaching reading in their classrooms. It is unrealistic to expect an untrained person to provide either the quality or quantity of reading instruction essential for today's youngsters. Yet, how is it possible to adequately train an aide in a procedure as intricate and complex as reading? While at first glance this task may seem insurmountable, with some planning and a great deal of perseverance the task can be accomplished.

FAMILIARIZING AIDES WITH READING INSTRUCTION

In its simplest terms reading is the act of comprehending meanings which are expressed in written language. Early man first learned to speak and later to represent his spoken language by means of a code. Written language, then, is a code for spoken language. Reading is the reverse process; that is, the translating or decoding of graphic symbols into the oral language. The decoding aspect of reading, therefore, requires that the reader perceive the separate sounds of the spoken language, then perceive the graphic symbols which represent the sounds, and finally relate the one to the other.

Obviously there is no one method that will miraculously teach every child to read. Children are individuals and therefore will learn individually, utilizing the approach or approaches most meaningful for them. Both teachers and aides must be familiar with a variety of reading approaches. The following are some of the most common methods by which children are taught to read.

The Basal Reading Approach

A basal reading program is built around a coordinated set of materials that provide both a systematic and sequential approach to the development of reading proficiency. This approach is characterized by its concern with growth in all aspects of the reading process including word attack, comprehension, and critical analysis. A basal reading approach focuses on three basic objectives in guiding development of the reading program — scope, sequence, and organization.

As with any reading approach, its effective use depends on the teacher. The basal reading approach provides such a variety of excellent materials that it is very easy for the teacher to follow the reading manual day after day, month after month. Thus, the teacher uses the basal approach as a foundation on which to build other reading experiences.

The Phonic Approach

The phonic approach to reading teaches word recognition as a sound-blending process. Under this method of instruction the youngster is taught beginning sounds of words, vowels and consonant sounds, and phonic blends. Proponents of this approach believe it helps to develop independence in recognizing new words and also helps the child see the association between printed letters and the speech sounds they represent.

In the actual methodology employed in the phonic approach the children are taught the sounds of letters and how to combine or synthesize them into words. The process always begins with individual letters and progresses to words. It continues with words that the children know; from these words generalizations are drawn on the basis of similar phonic elements, and then new words are introduced using these elements.

Initial Teaching Alphabet Approach

The initial teaching alphabet (ITA) is not really a method of reading instruction but rather a tool to be used by the teacher regardless of any approach she chooses. It is simply what the name implies, an alphabet. ITA is designed to simplify beginning reading by eliminating the discrepancies between the forty or so sounds in the English language and the more than 2,000 varied spellings that represent these sounds. A one-to-one relationship between letters seen and speech sounds heard is the result. There is only one letter character for each sound.

After she overcomes the difficulty of learning the unfamiliar initial teaching alphabet, the teacher's main role is implementing the alphabet into the total reading program. This alphabet is used only for beginning readers. The teacher must decide when each child is reading well enough in ITA to transfer him to the traditional material.

Language Experience Approach

This approach to reading instruction recognizes that learning to read is dependent on a child's oral language background. It recognizes the close relationship that exists among listening, speaking, reading, and writing. The language experience approach is built on the premise that the child's experiences in the various language arts before he enters school and during his school years are a determining factor in how well he will progress in his reading. Youngsters are unable to cope with either ideas or language in a reading program which is advanced beyond their own listening and speaking vocabulary.

The method used in teaching by the language experience approach is usually stated as follows:

What I can think about, I can talk about.

What I can say, I can write.

What I can write, I can read.

The child learns to read his own thoughts as they are written down by the teacher or aide. In implementing this program the teacher should encourage the child to share his ideas and experiences through oral expression. In time the child will be able to write stories with less and less help from the teacher or the aide. He can then read his own stories to the class and can eventually read the stories other children have written. Furthermore, he will be motivated to want to read standard reading stories from basal readers and the library.

The Linguistic Approach

In essence most linguistic programs for reading begin with language activities. The alphabet letters, both capital and lowercase forms, are learned. Words are introduced in spelling patterns. Sentences are then formed using words previously learned in the patterns.

The classroom teacher applies some of the basic linguistic principles by (1) providing experiences so that the child is aware that reading is really familiar talk written down on paper, and (2) using the beginning reading materials only after the child has shown signs of fluency in his own conversation of the words he will be reading. The linguistic reader focuses on words rather than isolated sounds. The teacher actually uses what could be called a whole-word approach in which the words are selected on the basis of their spelling patterns. Teachers are encouraged to have children do a great deal of writing, using word patterns they have read.

The Individualized Reading Approach

Individualized instruction in reading usually emphasizes the role of the teacher as a diagnostician and prescriber. The teacher must have goals outlined and skills identified before beginning a program. Skills can be taught to a single child, to a group, or to a whole class. Children are placed in short-term groups on the basis of their skill needs. Once the skill is mastered and the application assured, that particular group is discontinued.

Each child selects his own reading material, paces himself, and keeps accurate records of his progress. Under this approach each youngster reads widely from materials of his own choice. Once or twice a week the teacher meets with the child individually for five or ten minutes. She uses the conference time to determine what the student has read since the last conference, to evaluate by means of careful questions the degree of comprehension, and to take note of special needs and difficulties. The teacher guides the child, to some extent, in his future choice of materials.

USING A BASIC SIGHT VOCABULARY LIST

Most classroom teachers will find their aide of particular value in working with children who need either initial or remedial instruction with sight vocabulary words. These word lists usually include most of the basic sight words that are needed for fluent reading. While there are a variety of sight word lists, the most widely used one is *The Dolch Basic Word List* (Garrard Publishing Company: Champaign, Il.). The *Dolch List* contains 220 words that make up 50 to 75 percent of all school reading material. The first step in both the initial teaching of reading or in remedial work at a later grade level is to see that each child can recognize these basic words instantly on sight.

Most teacher aides can be quickly taught how to utilize a word list to help children improve reading skills. For example, the words can be written on flash cards by the aide and used with individual students who need additional vocabulary assistance. Using the basic approach the teacher or aide would take cards from the top of a stack at approximately one card per second and turn them over. If the child missed the word or hesitated, the card would be placed in another pile. The purpose of this process is to determine the sight vocabulary words known by the child.

Following the above procedure the teacher or aide can teach the child the unknown words. Most reading authorities recommend teaching three unknown words at a time to a slow learner and five to seven words at a time to a faster learner. Tell the child each unknown word and have him repeat it while looking at the word on the flash card. Then mix the cards containing the unknown words and show them to the student once again, having him name the words as rapidly as he can. If needed, repeat the telling, the shuffling, and the showing until he knows all of the previously unknown words.

An alternative approach, which could easily be supervised by an aide, would be to have two children play a game with the basic sight vocabulary cards. The first child, referred to as "the player," is to learn the words and the second child, who knows all of the words, is called "the helper." The player runs through the pack rapidly, handing each card to the helper as he calls it aloud; the helper then takes out any unknown or miscalled words. The helper then teaches these words to the player, shuffles the new words, and repeats the entire process. Finally, the helper mixes the new words with a larger number of old ones and has the player call them off rapidly with the player handing each card to the helper. Once again any unknown words are taken out.

ORAL READING

Oral reading is a process abounding in potential for both the teacher and the learner. For you and your aide oral reading can serve as a basis for diagnosis, for sharing with the students our literary heritage, and for presenting a model for children to emulate. For the student oral reading can provide opportunities to enhance the meaning of poetry and literature, to stimulate higher levels of thought, and to encourage the process of self-evaluation.

Teachers who use oral reading techniques successfully feel that they contribute to the child's development in a variety of ways. First of all, oral reading performance gives you a quick and accurate way of appraising certain key reading skills, such as word recognition and phrasing. It also serves to identify specific words and word recognition techniques on which help is needed. Secondly, oral reading assists in the development of good speech practices. Through oral reading a student can carry on a great deal of effective speech improvement. Thirdly, oral reading gives the learner practice in communicating to the entire group. Also, it can serve as an effective vehicle for dramatizing stories. And, finally, oral reading is an activity in which personality characteristics such as shyness and embarrassment are clearly evident and serves as a medium in which you can help youngsters toward better social adjustment.

If oral reading is to realize its potential as an effective learning tool, one prerequisite is essential. The reading material must be appropriate to the tasks and to the learner. For example, the story content should have been created for the human voice, such as in a play, poetry, etc.; and the readability should be suitable to the child's level of learning. In all instances, except diagnostic reading, oral reading should be prepared reading. Further, if a child is insecure in oral reading, it may be wise to select material at his independent rather than his instruction level.

Once you have made the decision regarding appropriate

material, there are a variety of ways you can utilize your aide to make oral reading a meaningful experience for youngsters in your classroom. For instance, it is desirable from time to time to have a diagnostic oral reading session with a child to check on his progress. While you are working with another reading group, you might have your aide take one child at a time to her desk and make a written record of errors, needs, etc., based on the child's performance in reading orally a fairly lengthy passage.

Under the right circumstances you might assign your classroom aide the task of working with a group of children on choral reading. This strategy will provide youngsters with an opportunity to perfect their oral reading ability. In choral reading the child, as one member of a group, has the security of learning from his more proficient classmates as he becomes one of them. Simple choral patterns which require only a few individual readings and a basic two-voice tone evolving from the meaning of the poem are promising introductory procedures.

Another kind of oral reading can provide an excellent way for children to share independent reading. A child is given the opportunity to read a particularly interesting selection to the class from something he has read independently. The child might practice with an aide until he can present it with fluency and good expression. Or, it might be advisable for you or the aide to listen to the child to make sure the reading is satisfactory before giving him a place in the oral reading schedule. An oral reading period once a week helps to motivate independent reading, provides an incentive for improving expression and speech, and affords an enjoyable listening experience.

STORYTELLING

One of life's rare moments for a child is when someone tells him a story. This is an effective teaching strategy we cannot afford to overlook. The benefits are too wide in range and too important in the total growth of the child to allow other activities to crowd out the "Story Hour." Through listening to carefully chosen stories children achieve growth in areas over and beyond the regular curriculum.

One of these areas, to which we often give too little thought, is that of feelings and emotions, an extremely important area if we really want to help children be well-rounded and sensitively aware individuals. The child's growing sense of values depends upon the way he feels about people and things. Few experiences can do more to promote this kind of growth in children than telling stories. The process can stretch children's minds, widen their viewpoints, push their horizons outward, and make them aware of the larger world which awaits them after they outgrow the small one in which they live. Through stories we can take them to faraway places and introduce them to various aspects of our own diverse society.

In your storytelling, if you make wise selections, you are introducing your children to literature. You should make sure that you include a wide range: folk tales, nursery rhymes, fiction, fact, and fantasy. If in your storytelling program you give children an interest in and love for reading and help them develop good taste in their choise of books, you will have given them something of lasting joy from which they will not depart.

There are numerous ways of telling stories. They can, for example, be read, acted out, told with puppets, and so on endlessly. Good storytelling is a highly creative and an extremely personal experience. In fact, good storytelling makes it possible for both the teller and the listener to participate. Together they can create a special world constructed with the words of the teller and the imagination of the listener. You can construct this world with one or fifty children, almost anywhere and at anytime, because the only things needed are your voice and the listener's imagination.

Before assigning storytelling tasks to a classroom aide it might be well to take stock of her personality and determine what types of stories she could tell in an effective manner. For example, if your aide is not the type of person who can act highly animated, steer her away from any stories that require her to make loud noises or weird sounds. Maybe she would enjoy telling animal stories, mystery stories with complicated plots, or stories of a humorous nature. Regardless of the kind of story you or the aide select, it should be exciting enough to make the aide want to tell the story to someone else.

Do not be surprised if your aide will need some assistance in perfecting storytelling skills. For instance, she may need to learn to use her vocal tones to full capacity. This may be difficult to do in the beginning, for most of us are rather shy, but with experience your aide will become more of a "ham." Likewise, she will need to practice using the rich, full scale of her voice. Most emotions can be conveyed by the tone of the voice. The speaker's intonation can change the meaning of a single word or an entire sentence.

The aide should also be reminded that she can create pictures with her words. Adjectives and adverbs are the kinds of words that are picturesque in storytelling. Encourage her to use them generously in her narative. They not only help the child visualize the story, but they appeal to his senses as well.

The hands are particularly important in storytelling. The hands can be used to convey or describe a variety of things — direction, size, weight, or distance. You may find that for some people using their hands is almost synonymous with talking; these individuals should be outstanding storytellers.

Remember, eye contact between the story teller and the listeners is important to an effective presentation. It gives a child the feeling that the entire story is being told just for him. Also, eyes play another important function in storytelling. When two or more characters in a story are talking, it helps the children to keep track of who is saying what if the aide's eyes move back and forth, each side representing a different character.

Finally, it is important to make any storytelling period a relaxed, informal time in the classroom. The storyteller should be very close to the children who are listening. Some teachers will gather the children around them, usually having them sit on the floor. Be sure to start each story session with some background about the setting for the story, facts about all the characters in the story, and any other preliminary comments necessary for understanding the story.

MOTIVATING INTEREST IN READING

The term *motivation* is used quite frequently by educators in connection with learning. Without student motivation little or no learning can take place in a reading program. Teacher aides can be especially helpful to teachers in creating a desire to read. While this is not a simple task, it is certainly not an impossible one either.

There are many procedures that teachers and aides can use to help children learn to enjoy reading. Basic to all of them of course is teaching children to read well enough so that the act of reading can be reasonably fluent and accurate and the content understood.

The more accessible books are, the greater the likelihood that they will be read. The classroom library should contain at least fifty different titles ranging from very easy to quite challenging, including a wide variety of topics from both fiction and nonfiction. A school librarian can give invaluable assistance to teachers in selecting books for classroom collections or for individual children.

Interest in reading can be both infectious and contagious. An aide who is enthusiastic about reading and who enjoys many children's books as well as adult books cannot help but convey some of the same enthusiasm to youngsters. Such an aide will call children's attention to new books when they arrive, perhaps reading just enough of the story to create interest; will help children to find books she feels they will enjoy reading; and will see that conditions are favorable for independent reading.

Quite often children differ with respect to the amount of encouragement they need to attack a learning task. If the teacher or aide fails to recognize the child's need, the child will stop working too soon and therefore fail to develop a sufficient attention span and qualities of persistence and diligence. The aide can help you by being sensitive to signs that a child needs encouragement. By simply patting a child on the back, making eye contact, or whispering a word she can encourage a reluctant learner.

In addition, children differ with respect to the amount, frequency, and kind of motivation they require for learning. Some have an inner drive for learning. They are eager to learn even if it is only for future reference. Other children must see a reason for every task which they confront. They must be convinced that what they are expected to learn has immediate relevance.

One of the best methods to motivate a reluctant learner to become an eager reader is to discover something that he is extremely interested in and then expose him to written information about his interest. Perhaps it is baseball. Track down all the books, magazines, and media materials you can find on the subject. More than likely, he will begin to see that there is at least one gratifying purpose in learning to read. Once you have interested him, it will be possible to teach him the skills he will need to read these materials.

Another technique which has been used with success by many teachers is to have an aide read a story to a child that he would not be able to read on his own. Besides increasing the child's store of knowledge, this technique will develop a greater interest in stories and literature and experiences that come from books. But best of all it will be sheer entertainment for the child and a wonderfully rewarding experience for the aide.

HELPING CHILDREN IN THE LIBRARY

Independent reading should be considered an important part of any reading program. Suitable materials for supplemental reading should be provided. A central library in a school with a trained librarian in charge is a valuable asset to a reading program. In addition, each classroom should have its own reading collection of at least fifty books, varying widely in difficulty, in content, and in style. Time for independent reading should be built into every teacher's classroom schedule, for supplemental reading allows children to read in a highly individualized way. Each child can set his own pace, select his own reading material, and proceed at his own rate.

Whether your school has classroom libraries or one central

library, the teacher aide can be an asset in teaching library skills to children. For example, youngsters will need to learn how to use the card catalog in locating books on the library shelves. Children need opportunities to practice locating information in card catalogs and to seek help from the aide when they are puzzled. The aide can show children how to utilize the catalog to answer the following questions about every book in the library:

- Where will I find a book with this title?
- Where in the library will I find books by this author?
- What books does the library have on this subject?
- Where will I find these books?

Likewise, there are many other kinds of reference materials with which youngsters should become acquainted before they finish elementary school. These include encyclopedias, atlases, almanacs, yearbooks, a biographical dictionary, a thesaurus, etc. If possible, the children should examine several kinds of each of these research tools. As introduction to each by a teacher or aide can open up a new avenue for independent learning. The teaching sequence of skills needed in locating information should include: (1) learning what types of information can be found in various reference works; (2) deciding under which heading or entries the information is likely to be found; and (3) locating the correct volume in works of more than one volume.

In addition to the general kinds of duties the aide may perform, the duties in regard to library activities could include:

1. Handling circulation routines — checking cards and renewing or checking out books
2. Assisting students in locating reference materials
3. Helping to set up audiovisual equipment for individual listening or viewing
4. Reviewing monthly periodicals and bulletins for items of interest to teachers
5. Checking shelves and making sure books are kept neatly in order
6. Making bibliographies on teacher request and putting books on reserve for teachers

PREPARING READING MATERIALS

Reading instruction probably places greater demands upon materials for large and small group activities than almost any other subject in the elementary school curriculum. Usually this increased demand for reading materials comes at the same time as the increased demand for planning time, creating all sorts of problems for the busy teacher. Here again, the effective utilization of a teacher aide can help solve the problem of reading material preparation.

Teacher aides can be assigned the task of securing materials pertaining to a particular skill you are planning to teach. In many cases it may mean that the aide will have to create the reading materials for you. Aides can be trained to translate teacher ideas into overhead transparencies, charts, or study guides. The aide may have to work for several hours constructing, copying, duplicating, counting, or sorting the materials needed for a five- or ten-minute presentation to an entire class. Obviously, you would not have time for all this preparation and still have time to teach throughout the day.

Materials with which children can reinforce and expand their sight vocabularies are especially useful to teachers who have a few children still reading at primary-grade levels. For supplementary small group practice, aides can construct flash cards. These can be large cards with words printed on them which can be used to present new words, to review words, to build phrases or sentences, and to increase speed of word recognition. Small cards are often employed for practice by individual children.

If you use an individualized teaching approach in your classroom, an instructional assistant can help you prepare or find suitable materials to implement the goals of this reading approach. Most research has shown that traditional materials, such as basal readers, are not organized to serve as functional tools for independent learning. To lack planning materials would place an unrealistic burden on you, especially if your classroom is in a demonstration school.

The amount of material needed in an individualized reading

program will depend largely on your ability to individualize learning experiences. Your aide can assist you in designing and preparing reading materials. For instance, she might help you prepare a study guide to help children master specific dictionary skills or construct task or job cards with each card giving sufficient information and directions to enable a youngster to work individually at a reading activity. Activity cards allow a student to choose the activities he is most interested in with the option of completing the cards in any sequence he desires.

If your aide is particularly talented in preparing materials, the two of you might prepare crossword puzzles, riddles, or even electric circuit quiz boards. If you are fortunate enough to have slides, filmstrips, tapes, or other media, by all means use them. Aide-made activity cards can ask youngsters to observe or listen to a relevant media presentation.

Much of your time and energy can be saved if materials are distributed in a businesslike and preplanned system. The aide can be assigned to distribute books or other materials at the proper time. If classroom drawers and supply cabinets are kept in excellent order, the aide will be able to get the materials quickly.

THE AIDE'S RESPONSIBILITIES

To the alert teacher every reading activity provides opportunities for her to become better acquainted with the reading performance of the children. An effectively trained teacher aide can help the teacher with this important task. For example, the aide can assist in discovering children who are finger pointing, have poor reading posture, are holding the book too close, or have lip movement while reading. Likewise, special strengths or weaknesses in comprehension can be observed as children try to answer questions of various kinds orally or in writing.

Some teachers like to prepare a file folder for each child in which reading records of various kinds can be kept while others prefer to use a loose-leaf notebook. Regardless of the kind of reading record you prefer, your aide can be a valuable asset in the record-keeping process. Keeping adequate reading records is a necessity if children are to be understood and treated as individuals. Record keeping can, however, become a heavy burden unless additional assistance is provided for classroom teachers.

Further, if we accept the idea that in order to encourage reading one needs to be well versed in content as well as in methods of instruction, the teacher aide needs more than a nodding acquaintance with children's books. To be an enthusiastic and convincing salesman for children's books the aide must be thoroughly familiar with these books. To bring children and books together effectively she should both understand the children and have a broad acquaintance with the books that might suit them. If the aide is to discuss children's reading with them in individual or group discussions, she should know the book well enough to ask intelligent questions about it. Reading children's books need not be a disagreeable chore for aides; a book that is good for children should also be an enjoyable experience for an adult who has not completely buried his childhood interests.

In addition, a classroom aide can participate in the following kinds of specific reading activities:

1. Read orally to children for the main purpose of enjoyment. This is also a time to develop comprehension skills at the oral level.
2. Listen to individual children read for the purpose of providing practice. Children usually enjoy oral reading and find adults very motivating.
3. Provide a model by echo reading with a child. The aide reads a sentence and the child immediately reads the same sentence patterning his reading after the aide's.
4. Construct games and activities for the reinforcement of sight words and phonic skill instruction.
5. Work with individual students who have been designated by the teacher as likely to encounter difficulty with a particular reading assignment.
6. Assist children in writing language experience stories. In this situation the child tells the story to the aide and she

writes the story for the child.

7. Evaluate the reading performance of selected children. Evaluation should begin with a word list test — either a published one such as the *Dolch Basic Word List* or a list compiled from the basal reader.

SUMMARY

Good organization is more essential for teaching reading than for almost any other curriculum area. Because children learn to read in a variety of ways, reading instruction demands that attention be given both to individual students and to small instructional groups. There are many effective teachniques for teaching children the basic skills in reading, but underlying each of them is the common need for well-planned, sequentially developed instruction. For these reasons, among others, the teacher aide can play a vital role in your reading program.

The success of your classroom aide will be dependent on your ability to establish a healthy working relationship with her. Your responsibility is to determine the structure of the reading instruction that will be most beneficial for your class. The aide's responsibility is to assist you in carrying out that instruction. The aide must constantly communicate with the teacher, providing information which is relevant to future instructional decisions. However, it is imperative that the aide recognize that instructional decisions for the reading program must be made by you, the classroom teacher.

CHAPTER 6

MULTIMEDIA RESPONSIBILITIES

THERE are few classrooms today where modern communication technology has not had an impact. In many cases students have been able to gain new insights through the use of filmstrips, tapes, television, and other audiovisual devices. In far too many classrooms audiovisual hardware is just another frustration in the teacher's day and another hurdle for the children to surmount in their quest for knowledge. Fortunately, even though the technology of communications is becoming more and more complex, the new communication devices are becoming simpler to operate and, as a result, offer more potential for use than ever before.

Hardly a day goes by that a new teaching device or an improvement over an older device does not appear on the market. The modern teacher needs to be aware of these devices as possible aids to her teaching. She should understand how these devices can best be utilized for maximum learning by her children. She should, however, avoid the widely held misconception that all media materials possess educative values. There are educational values in films, filmstrips, records, tapes, bulletin boards, etc. only where these devices are used wisely in the teaching-learning process.

Media instruction has demonstrated its importance in the teaching-learning process. Yet many teachers who feel they lack specific training have been driven by feelings of insecurity to shy away from the use of any mechanical devices. Teacher aides who are familiar with the operation and potential use of such equipment can bring a much-needed skill to the classroom.

ORIENTATION AND TRAINING

Some educators have suggested that one of the first responsibilities that should be given to a new teacher aide is the task of working with media equipment. In such a case it might be wise during either the orientation period or the opening days of the school year to acquaint your aide with your own philosophy concerning media utilization. The authors have seen many ludicrous examples of the misuse of multimedia equipment and materials. For example, some teachers use them simply for entertainment or classroom control. Other teachers fail to use media materials at all, believing that their use is an unnecessary frill. Regardless of the approach you favor, it will be to your advantage to discuss your media plans with your new instructional assistant.

The next step should be to acquaint your aide with multimedia equipment available in your school. While each school will have its own varied mixture of equipment, the following items are common examples of equipment found in most elementary schools:

Motion picture projectors
Filmstrip projectors
Tape recorders
Slide projectors
Overhead projectors
Opaque projectors
Maps and globes
Language labs

Once you have familiarized your aide with the available media equipment (usually referred to as *hardware*), you will want to make her aware of media software. The term *software* refers to the educational materials available for each piece of equipment — slides for the projector, tapes for the recorders, etc. Normally, such software is found in either the school library or the media center. Almost all software items are catalogued in bulletins readily available to the aide.

After having developed a working knowledge of the equipment, particularly of those machines favored by the teacher, the next task at hand is for the aide to learn how to operate each of the machines efficiently and to perform limited repair operations. Proper operation of multimedia equipment can make or break a particular presentation. Not having the equipment ready on time, fumbling its operation, or causing breakdowns by mishandling can completely destroy the effectiveness of media presentations. Fortunately for those of us who are not mechanically inclined, the operation of most multimedia devices has been simplified, and a few minutes practice on each machine should provide reasonable mastery.

The best way to insure a good working knowledge of equipment in the classroom is to reserve some practice time for aides. It obviously takes practice to thread and rewind a projector or to operate a tape recorder efficiently. If at all possible make sure a couple of practice sessions are arranged with someone who possesses a knowledge of the equipment. A mistake made in a practice session is one less mistake performed in the classroom before a group of restless children.

In addition to operating media equipment and assisting you in the selection of proper software, your aide should also be trained in the procedures for scheduling presentations. Schools usually have a check-out and reservation procedure for multimedia equipment. Some of the most heated arguments between teachers have occurred over who reserved what piece of equipment and when. Most of these conflicts could have been avoided if teachers and aides had followed routine reservation procedures.

Always be careful to make sure that the equipment you reserve is picked up and returned on time by your teacher aide. Such promptness insures the maximum efficient use of the equipment by the entire faculty. Nothing is more disconcerting to a class of students than waiting with nothing to do for a multimedia presentation. Such slack time can lead to disciplinary problems as well as inhibit the effectiveness of the presentation.

You might want to give some consideration to the following guidelines as you provide experience for your teacher aide in utilizing media:

1. Always demonstrate the use of films or filmstrips with the class before you ask your aide to use these media in your classroom.

2. Emphasize the need for previewing all media software before using them with the class.
3. Explain in detail the procedure for securing films and filmstrips from your school's media center.
4. Encourage your aide to check all equipment before she expects to use it.
5. Provide your aide the time needed to locate, preview, and set up for the use of films or filmstrips.

MEDIA UTILIZATION PROCEDURES

Educational media are designed to enhance and further learning objectives. After you have identified the major concepts to be taught, you and your aide can proceed in developing activities which may accomplish your objectives. Being aware of media and having access to a variety of different types of media equipment are essential to effective classroom instruction.

Definitely, the purpose for which media materials are to be used is the most important consideration when it comes to selection. A review of your curriculum guide and the lesson plans you have used in the past will give you an idea of which new materials you can use to clarify difficult points and to amplify areas which need more emphasis. Having determined these needs you are now ready to consider which materials best meet them.

Next, you should arrange to preview any materials that appear to serve your instructional purposes. Today most schools have special facilities available for this function. A critique of each medium presentation previewed, whether ultimately used or not, is useful for future reference. A preview is essential to the development of a good classroom media program.

In evaluating new materials you need to ask yourself one important question: Will this teaching aid help my students learn something in a better, more lasting way? If your answer is a tentative *yes*, put the materials to the test. However, be prepared to drop any media materials which obviously do not work. Give any new teaching aid a chance to work. Be sure you understand how to use it, and use it long enough to be certain of the results you are getting.

Effective timing is another critical aspect of media preplanning. At what point during the instructional process should the multimedia materials be introduced? For example, some materials are most effectively used in introducing a lesson; others should be used as, or along with, the heart of a lesson; a few may be best utilized as culmination activities.

Usually audiovisual materials and equipment must be reserved several days in advance. However, it is often impossible to predict precisely how quickly students will progress, thus creating some problems in scheduling. Some schools purchase all media materials as one way of overcoming some of the timing problems. Sometimes a film or tape does not arrive as scheduled. Occasionally a film projector breaks down, and so on. Thus, it becomes imperative to prepare alternative activities for every scheduled use of media. This is not a particularly difficult task, but it is one that is frequently neglected by teachers.

The introductory comments preceding the utilization of media materials should be designed to prepare students for what they will experience. Usually two or three key questions should be posed. Rather than emphasizing facts, the questions should focus upon relationships, applications, or hidden meanings. Sometimes certain problems or problem situations should be noted. At other times new terms or new ideas should be pinpointed. Too many questions or points to look for may be confusing.

Once the medium has been used, the next step is the follow-through discussion to determine how well the original questions were answered. Attention should be directed to any incorrect notions or unanticipated misunderstandings which may have resulted. Sometimes differences between the medium source presently being used and information from other sources may conflict or at least appear to do so. Above all, students should be encouraged to pose their own questions for reflection. Sometimes students' questions will suggest the need for additional media materials, or they may suggest the need for other kinds of class activities.

MEDIA CENTER

The trend in recent years has been to set aside a portion of the school facility to serve as a media center. Usually these centers contain audiovisual materials, tapes, slides, books, and other reference materials. Also science materials, maps, cassettes, films, and charts may be stored here. There is also an implied need for viewing rooms, conference rooms, and individual study carrels equipped with electrical outlets to permit the use of various machines and other media hardware.

Traditionally, the school library has been considered the learning laboratory of an effective school; now the modern, well-equipped media center serves in the same capacity. When properly managed, the center provides not only a place where the student may read, but also a place where he may see, listen, and perform. However, maximum use of the center is possible only when teachers and aides are thoroughly familiar with all the available resources.

There are a variety of ways in which students may be motivated to make extensive use of the media center. The following methods may prove useful: (1) school assemblies featuring the media center and facilities, (2) periodic bulletins announcing new materials and equipment available, (3) using the media center for special occasions such as Open House or PTA meetings, and (4) preparation of special racks to display new materials or to highlight special seasons. Perhaps the most effective way to stimulate use of the media center is to provide the kind of materials and services that will provide students with rewarding experiences.

Maximum use of the media center is possible only if students and members of the staff are familiar with the services offered. Aides can assist you in providing meaningful instruction to students on the use of the media center. In some cases members of the media staff may plan regular visits to your classroom. The major advantage of this plan is that it acquaints students with the media staff and motivates teachers and aides to stimulate children to make wider use of the services and facilities. However, the demands of modern media centers are such that they cannot be met by the professional staff alone. Most educators agree that it is uneconomical to use professionally trained personnel to perform tasks that can be done by competent aides. It is common practice to use aides as assistants in the media center. Among the duties that media aides can perform are returning books to the shelves, assisting at the charge desk, delivering audiovisual materials, filing films and slides, doing minor equipment repair, and arranging bulletin boards.

The experience that aides gain can be most worthwhile, but it is necessary that they be given effective supervision in planning their work and be assigned tasks that will contribute to the education of children in your classroom. Routine media tasks soon lose their challenge if variety is not provided in daily assignments. Also, there should be some attempt to assist aides in developing good work habits and in learning from their experiences. Only through proper training and systematic planning is it possible to make effective use of media aides.

MATERIALS PREPARATION

With relatively little advanced training and with simple directions from teachers, aides can prepare such media items as charts, models, overhead transparencies, tapes, and picture files. This preparation of *software* is vital to the development of an effective classroom multimedia program.

Important sources of training for aides in the preparation of media materials are the commercial enterprises which sell the hardware equipment used in most classrooms. Many of these manufacturers offer evening or Saturday workshops for both the professional staff and teacher aides. Usually this service is free, and most of the training is of excellent quality. Other important sources of training in materials preparation are curriculum centers at nearby universities and colleges. Many educational departments in institutions of higher learning now include courses on preparation and use of media materials in their basic curriculum. More than likely, teacher aides would be welcome to take these courses. In addition, if your school district has a media specialist, he or she could be another important source of training in this field.

To the greatest extent possible aides should be utilized in preparing audiovisual materials. For instance, one inexpensive, easy-to-use, and highly successful aid is the write-on slide. This film is a specially treated, clear slide which is coated so that it can be drawn on or written upon and can be projected using a regular slide projector. Although the best images are obtained with drawing ink made specially for use on drafting film, images can be formed using almost any pencil or felt-tip pen. Transfer letters may also be used.

Write-on slides can be used by teachers or aides for review questions, to show diagrams, and as flash cards. Other teachers have used these slides as illustrations to accompany oral reports; as drill and skill activities for early readiness training; as phonics review slides for independent study; as follow-up activities after field trips; and as individual expression around a specific theme. Creative teachers and aides should be able to find many other uses for such a flexible, yet inexpensive, teaching aid.

In addition, an intelligent and creative aide, planning a teaching unit under the direction of the teacher, can make many materials for the overhead projector. Most of these transparencies can be created from line drawings or from typewritten masters and prepared on any duplicating machine. The aide can, with assistance from the teacher, make drawings, type lines of poetry, produce problems, and reproduce other items on standard mimeograph paper. These reproductions can be mounted on separate cardboard frames using masking tape or special mounting materials.

Other materials you might consider having your aide construct might include science charts and folders explaining experiments, word charts, and listening tapes. Pretaped stories and lessons to be filed in a listening center can be of great assistance to slow learners. Tapes have many additional advantages. They can be used for small group or individual drill, for students who are ill and miss practice in basic processes, and for those who need special help.

EVALUATING INSTRUCTIONAL MATERIALS

The first characteristic to be considered by a teacher in selecting learning aids is relevancy to the goal-seeking activity involved. Generally, if a rich classroom environment is provided, learning will be facilitated. In addition, the choice of materials and resources should be based upon the purposes, background, and maturity of the class. Too often media presentations are selected on bases other than the objectives to be achieved and the needs of the students to be taught.

The array of equipment available to assist the classroom teacher is almost beyond comprehension. Much of what is available is good; however, some of it is useless. Choosing the kind of equipment to be used is not always an easy job. For example, instructional hardware should be purchased with explicit instructional goals in mind. The idea that it is extremely stylish to own an 8 mm loop projector or the notion that an instructional program will be improved if a piece of equipment is "available" is both foolish and naive. Rather than purchasing media hardware and accompanying software merely to superimpose them on the existing curriculum, you must think of and select new hardware as an integral part of an improved instructional plan.

Record players, tape recorders, film projectors, etc. must be purchased with the user in mind. Much of this type of equipment has been purchased on the basis of a low bid with little attention given to adequate specifications. As a result such equipment usually lies dormant in storage cabinets because no one understands how to use it.

In making use of new media you should note why you prefer one medium over another. Is it ease of operation, ready access, availability of appropriate software? Why is it that more teachers do not use films, slides, or tapes? Is the equipment too hard to operate or too heavy? Is there no software to meet existing needs? Such comments should be forwarded to your principal or media coordinator who, we hope, will consider your evaluation when ordering new equipment.

The purpose for which media materials are to be used is the

most important consideration when it comes to selection. A review of your grade-level curriculum guide and the lesson plans you have used in the past will give you an idea of what new materials you can use to clarify difficult points and to amplify areas which have received little emphasis in the past. Having determined these instructional needs you are now ready to consider materials to fulfill them.

Your principal or school district purchasing agent should be able to give you accurate, up-to-date information on the new kinds of materials currently available in elementary education. In addition, a look through catalogs of educational materials, advertisements in professional magazines, and discussions with fellow teachers can help you locate helpful teaching aids.

Regardless of the evaluation procedure you choose, the best test may well be simply trying the materials out on your own students, observing the results, and making your own decision. Be prepared to quickly drop any materials which obviously do not work, but give any new medium aid a chance to work. Be sure you understand how to use the aid, then use it long enough to be sure of exactly what kind of results you are getting. Some informal pre- and posttesting will help you determine your results.

The sample checklist developed by the authors will aid teachers in evaluating their effectiveness in using multimedia materials.

HOW'S YOUR M-Q*

Score one point for each *Yes*

1. Do you utilize media material in a regular classroom setting, avoiding large group presentations (two or more classes together)? _____
2. Do you utilize only media materials that serve the needs of your students and are pertinent to current instructional objectives? _____
3. Do you always preview the media presentation prior to using it with your entire class? _____
4. Do you introduce the film to your class — indicating points to look for and explaining difficult words used in the film? _____
5. Do you operate all media equipment carefully in order to avoid damage? _____
6. Do you make it a point to never leave any media equipment while it is running? _____

7. Do you always have films threaded and the title in focus prior to your introductory remarks? _____
8. Do you know where to locate replacement parts for media equipment in your building? _____
9. Do you allow sufficient time for class discussion of information contained in the media presentation? _____
10. Do you immediately return all media equipment and materials to their proper location? _____

HOW DO YOU RATE:

10 points = Professional
9 points = Excellent
8 points = Capable
7 points = Inconclusive
6 points
or less   = Hide your score

*Media Quotient

TIPS ON BULLETIN BOARDS

Attractively presented materials coupled with thought-provoking questions can stimulate children's interest in learning. Bulletin boards and classroom displays offer this enjoyable aid to children's learning. A teacher aide can contribute a great deal by brightening a classroom with creative, attractive, and informative bulletin boards.

Bulletin boards are utilized for a variety of purposes — teaching units are introduced, student work is displayed, units are culminated, and special events and holidays are noted. Many teachers have found that bulletin boards can be used as a means of individualizing instruction while giving all the children an opportunity to look, react, and learn.

The challenge of change has shown that bulletin boards can and should be more than simply artwork. This is not to say that bulletin boards should not be artistic, neat, and appealing, but most of all they should be meaningful to the students. Students should share in their planning and development, for as we involve children in the teaching-learning process, all classroom activities can be reevaluated to insure maximum student participation.

The following are suggestions for setting up a bulletin board or display. The most effective learning bulletin boards are jointly planned and arranged by children, teachers, and aides working together.

1. Decide on the learning concepts or principles you wish children to learn.
2. Teachers, aides, and children will then collect pictures from magazines, newspapers, or prepared materials which they think might help in teaching these concepts.
3. The teacher (and aide if possible) plans how the pictures can be used effectively and attractively on a bulletin board display. Also, decide upon thought-provoking questions.
4. Make diagrams if needed to supplement the pictures.
5. Have your aide prepare the lettering and materials needed for the display. This may entail pasting pictures on colored paper, etc.
6. The posting of the display may be done by children under the supervision of a teacher or aide.
7. After the display has served its purpose, it may be taken down and stored in a folder or envelope for possible use and modification next year.

It is important to remember that displays generally have an advantage over certain bulletin boards because they allow the children to tinker with the materials that are set out. Tactile stimulation through the use of their sense of touch is very desirable for most children.

DEFINING THE AIDE'S ROLE

Your teacher aide can make a real difference in your media program if you are imaginative enough to utilize your aide well. Only through a true partnership of teacher and aide can real service to children be increased. "How can we as a team help the children in your classroom?" is a good question with which to begin each school day.

All aides will need some orientation in the operation of special equipment which will be used to generate materials for teachers. Staff members should be able to train an artistically talented aide in the use of materials necessary to make, for instance, transparencies for overhead projectors, graphs and charts for science and mathematics, and models and educational games for other areas of the elementary curriculum. One or more of the school's aides could be trained by some staff members or by a community volunteer to operate a movie camera or to use darkroom equipment.

An aide's multimedia tasks could include the following:

- Preparing posters, charts, and other visual aids through dry mounting
- Laminating visual teaching aids
- Checking out and returning films, tapes, etc.
- Making transparencies for the overhead projector
- Working with photography equipment and developing film
- Preparing spirit masters and stencil masters
- Setting up and operating tape recorders, filmstrip projectors, opaque projectors, etc.
- Writing to companies and organizations for free media materials
- Preparing classroom bulletin boards and displays
- Collecting pictures and other materials for class work
- Keeping inventory of all media equipment in the building
- Providing information to aid teachers in the selection of new software
- Giving assistance to students who are working on media projects
- Supervising live videotaping in the classroom
- Keeping media equipment in good condition (cleaning, changing lamps, etc.)
- Operating the Thermo-Fax® machine when requested

SUMMARY

Our society is becoming more and more dependent upon communication hardware. It is rare indeed to find a home without a telephone or a television set. Few homes lack a camera of some type. Teachers must stop thinking of technology as something that might replace them. It is time that we muster all of our resources — hardware, software, and human — to meet the challenge of educating children.

Paramount in the success of any media program is the selection of the right kind of instructional hardware and the provision of a proper environment for its effective use. While the classroom teacher is a key person in this process, she must have the constant help and support from aides throughout her school to be effective. Only with assistance from the teacher aide can a media program become an integral part of your classroom instructional process.

CHAPTER 7

THE TEACHER AIDE
OUTSIDE THE CLASSROOM

M OST elementary schools have found that teacher aides can be of service to children in areas beyond the classroom. For instance, aides are eagerly welcomed by teachers when they assist with such routine, but necessary, tasks as supervising the playground, cafeteria, and corridors. This additional assistance not only permits teachers to devote more of their energies to classroom activities but provides children with an opportunity to interact with another adult.

However, teachers and administrators should make every effort to effectively train an aide prior to assigning her tasks outside the classroom. Often teachers assume that since such tasks do not require instructional expertise or experience, aides will be able to supervise without specific training or detailed instructions. An aide should not be assigned supervisory duties outside the classroom by herself until she has displayed an ability to effectively handle any situation which might arise. If an aide assigned to an area does not know how to handle the assignment, serious problems can and probably will develop sooner or later.

Most elementary schools have a rather elaborate system of rules and regulations to cover the activities of children in areas outside the regular classroom. It is your responsibility as a teacher to make sure that teacher aides under your supervision are cognizant of school regulations. Failure to meet this responsibility could cause you to be liable under certain circumstances for injuries sustained by children on the playground or in the cafeteria.

This duty should not be thought of as simply "policing" or an unpleasant task. Rather, the playground is a vital and interesting part of the school. Here youngsters carry on much of their social life and learn how to get along with other children.

The school cafeteria also provides another opportunity for children to socialize. It is an integral part of every elementary school, and learning takes place here as well as in the classroom.

SUPERVISING THE PLAYGROUND

Children need an environment with many sensory and social experiences to facilitate learning. The playground is a wonderful means of enriching their lives and interacting with them as they grow and develop. Playground activities also help children learn to communicate by expressing ideas and feelings through physical movement and verbal interchange. Youngsters learn to compete as well as to cooperate. They develop skills and understandings which enhance their self-confidence, and they experience and internalize such concepts as fast, slow, up, down, over, under. They learn in a laboratory of "doing" how to listen, communicate, follow directions, and relate to their peers as well as to adults.

Children should always have some freedom to select the physical activities they wish to pursue. Without the freedom of choice to build their own performance systems children may not obtain the wide range of benefits possible from their physical play. However, granting this freedom does not mean that we should leave youngsters entirely to their own devices. It means first of all that there must be adequate and appropriate equipment designed to meet the children's developing skills and interests. It also means that the playground facilities and environment should provide optimal physical response under the guidance of adults.

The supervision of playground activities can often be a very complex task. At the same time it can also be a very exciting, enjoyable, and rewarding experience for a teacher aide. An observant aide will learn much about youngsters by watching them approach certain physical activities on the playground. Some children will revert to more primitive motor patterns as they go up steps or climb on an apparatus. A child may have difficulty with balance, tend to bump into things, or run with his feet spread wide apart. It is interesting to watch children at play and note how they pace themselves for both activity and rest.

By close observation an aide can get to know a lot about the student in his natural environment. She can learn if he is a leader or follower or whether he is popular or unpopular with other children. She might ask herself such questions as these: Does he display a friendly or hostile attitude toward his playmates? Is he gifted in physical abilities or athletic play? Supervision also presents the opportunity for aides to develop friendships with children outside the classroom. Often friendships made under these circumstances provide new relationships within the classroom environment. A casual friendship developed on the playground may help a youngster to see the aide in an entirely different light.

However, if your teacher aide is to be an effective playground supervisor, there are a variety of questions that must be answered for her. For example:

1. Where can children play, and what areas of the school grounds are off limits?
2. Is there any play equipment available? If so, who distributes and collects it?
3. What is the aide to do in case of an emergency? Who is to be notified?
4. Under what conditions can youngsters reenter the school building during play time?
5. What kind of professional help is available to aides on the playground?
6. What procedures should be followed when fights occur on the playground?
7. What is the length of the play period? Are children required to line up to come into the building?
8. How do the children know when the recess period has ended?

In addition, teacher aides should be made aware of any safety hazards present on the playground. It is important to remember that even one school accident is one too many. Constant vigilance on the part of teachers and aides can pay high dividends in such areas as the health and safety of school children. Many safety hazards may be only seasonal. For example, rain can produce slippery sidewalks; wind can turn doors into dangerous, moving objects; ice can create obvious possibilities for slipping and sliding. Even certain times of the school day can increase the potential for injury to youngsters. Students running for a bus after school or children eager to be first in line when reentering the building after recess can easily create hazards for themselves as well as others.

Aides should also be forewarned of the hazard that heavy vehicle traffic causes for children playing on the school grounds. One careless error here could easily cost a student his life. It is often helpful for teachers and aides to station themselves between children at play and the nearby street. In addition, youngsters should be constantly reminded of the dangers posed by street traffic.

If aides are to be given direct authority over children on the playground, they should be aware of procedures to follow when fights between students occur. An effective teacher knows that most fights can be stopped before they are started if the adult on duty can anticipate trouble and take corrective steps. Friendly shoving may often turn into a fight. A shouting match can quickly develop into a more serious problem. However, if a fight does develop in an aide's supervisory area, she should be instructed not to panic. Instead, she should try to provide a calm example for the children to follow. It is important for her to keep the other children from becoming involved in the fracas. If the combatants refuse to stop, the aide should immediately enlist the help of a teacher. Failure to use appropriate discretion during a disturbance may be disastrous for the teacher aide.

In working with teacher aides in regard to playground supervision it is suggested that they be provided with the following basic principles:

1. Always be punctual for the duty assignment.
2. Circulate — do not stay in one location all the time.
3. Do not make threats which you cannot possibly carry

out.

4. Know your area of responsibility on the playground.
5. Check your play area for any possible safety hazards.
6. Do not join in games with the children on a daily basis since this practice can limit your field of supervision.
7. Do not let teachers or other aides monopolize your time through excessive socializing.
8. Know what to do in emergency situations.
9. Utilize the supervisory opportunity to improve your classroom relationships.
10. Be constantly alert while on duty.

ORGANIZING GAMES AND ACTIVITIES

Nothing strikes fear in elementary teachers more than the principal's announcement that weather conditions require indoor recess. However, for teachers with a little imagination and initiative there is a whole world of activities awaiting their students in their own classrooms. Aides can be valuable colleagues in conducting indoor games and activities.

Rhythm activities are probably as simple to provide as any. By simply pushing desks and other classroom furniture to the sides or to the back of the room and placing a record on a record player you can get your youngsters involved in such activities as square dancing or folk dancing. Lummi sticks offer another means for rhythmic activity in your classroom. Students can use the small stick — approximately a foot long and a half inch or so in diameter — in any number of routines. They can tap the floor to the sound of music, pass the stick around the room, flip them to a partner, etc. Lummi sticks offer almost endless creative, rhythmic possibilities and are easy to make out of old broomsticks or mop handles.

Another good classroom activity is jumping rope. Again, various routines can be developed. Also, hoops laid next to each other on the floor make for good hopping, jumping, and high-stepping practice, as well as a means of playing games. Good hoops can be constructed from a flexible plastic pipe or hose. The hoops can be made into different sizes, but those with a circumference of 7 to 10 feet are most useful. Moving in space without equipment is enjoyable too. Walking, running, jumping, hopping, skipping, moving high or low, fast or slow, forward or backward — all of these help a child to understand and express himself.

You or your aide could quarter the room off and play balloon volleyball. A dozen or so balloons can lead to an interesting session. You might choose to let the children develop their own rules until they find how to enjoy the game the most. Many teachers also find that as skill develops, so do the rules. Exercises in writing can also be stressed by simply having the youngsters record a description of the game and rules by which to play.

Three-by-five balance rails can be set up on small wooden blocks, offering a variety of balance challenges for elementary students. Tin can stilts can do likewise. Sit-ups and other physical exercises can also be used. A series of stations can be set up in your room where rope jumping is going on at one, hoop work in another, ball bouncing in another, and so on.

There are many other activities that a teacher and aide can devise with just a classroom at their command. A relay game in which participants blow a table tennis ball 6 feet is just as exciting as one in which they run 100 feet. A tournament with four sets of Chinese Checkers® can occupy a class during indoor recess for an entire rainy week. How about bowling by rolling a softball at milk cartons? Youngsters can play basketball by tossing paper balls at a wastebasket or box. Miniature golf can be played on a carpet strip using plastic practice golf balls and a ring of clay as a target. It does not take much to do most of these activities. Teachers and aides with a little imagination, some initiative, and the willingness to move their desks aside can embark on some fascinating physical activities right in their own classroom.

Quieter activities could include reading from a growing classroom library or books for enjoyment and encouragement. Easels for painting along with large jars and brushes should be handy. Both boys and girls are interested in handicrafts such as weaving and papier-mâché; making puppets or kites is also an excellent indoor activity.

Dramatic play is another area of great interest. Children like to build stage sets and to follow through on every detail from costumes and props to program printing. At a young age many children begin to become very skillful at making and using hand puppets and marionettes. As the children gain in mathematical skill, there is greater interest in board games involving three or four players.

Play groups help children to learn how to get along with each other and to develop concepts of fair play and good sportsmanship. They also begin to learn the values of concentration as well as quick and accurate thinking. Not the least among the values of playing games are the many possible learning experiences involving such subjects as literature, science, history, and art.

When working with games and activities you should always remember to work in close cooperation with your teacher aide. Neither of you should forget your responsibilities for the safety of the children in your charge. Always be sure that classroom conditions are such that no student subjects himself to any unnecessary risk. In your classroom the slogan, *Safety First*, should always be followed by both you and your teacher aide.

SUPERVISING IN THE SCHOOL CAFETERIA

The supervision of the school cafeteria can often be a touchy matter. If your school has a cafeteria, problems may often focus here. Running to secure a place in line or pushing and shoving to move ahead are all common occurrences. Children tend to be careless and often throw litter and debris on the cafeteria floor. This room is, without doubt, one of the most difficult places to contain children for any length of time.

To cope with this situation most schools require aides to help supervise the children during the cafeteria period. However, for an aide to be successful, she should be firm but friendly. When children approach the cafeteria they are usually anxious to socialize with their classmates and are full of youthful energy. More often than not, they will be giddy and excited. If the aide is the type of individual who gets upset by the first overturned tray, then she is in the wrong place.

Some ground rules must be established by administrators if the school cafeteria is to be effectively supervised by teacher aides. Answers to the following kinds of questions must be supplied to aides who are assigned to cafeteria duty:

- What are the rules for student conduct in the cafeteria?
- How long must children remain in the cafeteria before they are dismissed?
- What kind of atmosphere does the staff want the cafeteria to reflect?
- What kind of authority does an aide have in the cafeteria?
- What should an aide do if a child becomes ill or is injured?
- What should the aide do if one or more children become unruly?

Too often, aides assigned to cafeteria duty forget that teaching proper behavior is a long process that requires much patience. Children will inevitably forget or ignore school rules and good manners. An aide will have to reteach proper behavior many times during the school year. It is to be hoped, however, that she will do this with the same patience that she exhibits in working with a slow reader.

Obviously, the first step in reteaching incorrect social behavior is recognizing and reacting to it, just as the first step in reteaching reading skills is recognizing and correcting errors made. Students expect adults to react to misbehavior if it disrupts the smooth operation of the cafeteria or the well-being of fellow students. Most children prefer firm maintenance of limits.

An aide needs to be reminded that a simple request to stop misbehavior can take many forms. She can give a meaningful glance, call the child's name, or simply touch his shoulder. Regardless of the form she uses, she should use it in the same spirit she corrects a mispronounced word in a reading class.

When students do not respond to simple requests to behave, teacher aides frequently raise their voices and scold the child. Such emotional outbursts rarely accomplish what the aide in-

tends. Aides who scold loudly and threaten are usually ineffective. Their warnings give pause the first few times children
hear them, but their words become progressively ineffective as
the scolding is repeated over and over.

Once on the job, your aide may find the following hints
helpful:

1. Keep cool. An aide who loses her temper does little to help
   a problem situation.
2. Know your area of supervison.
3. Make sure you are highly visible to students at all times.
4. Do not stand in one place all the time.
5. If a potential trouble spot is observed, go to it immediately.
6. If a dangerous situation develops, send for help immediately.
7. Think positive thoughts.

HELPING WITH FIELD TRIPS

At some time every teacher has been involved in a school
field trip or excursion. Typically such a trip may be seen by the
students as a holiday from school and by the teacher as a series
of management difficulties with twenty-five students. Through
adequate planning, however, a field trip can be an invaluable
and enjoyable learning experience for all.

If field trips are to be a valuable learning experience, the
excursion should be planned in relation to ongoing instructional activities within the classroom. Field trips can be a
means of enriching the youngsters' study by letting them participate in learning experiences which are not easily visualized
through the ordinary methods of reading assignments or group
discussions. Often field trips are taken near the beginning of a
unit for the purpose of gathering information on specific topics
or problems. On other occasions trips may serve as part of the
actual teaching of the unit so that the students may get fresh
motivation and acquire expanded background for their study.
In addition, field trips may also serve as a culminating activity
for a particular topic of study with the purpose of synthesizing

all the gathered information into a comprehensible whole. Whenever the field trip is taken, it should be closely related to the classroom activities and instructional objectives or requirements.

Varied and valuable insights are achieved through participation in field trips aside from the mere fact gathering and first-hand observation activities. As the children plan together and socialize with one another, the many activities that they experience make an important contribution by broadening and enriching the entire group's social skills and values. Therefore, an important fringe benefit of field trips is the socialization that takes place among the children as they discuss their observations, sit together on the bus, ask questions of the guide, and write their impressions.

Successful field trips demand that extraordinary care should be taken in planning properly and thoroughly. The teacher and aide should make reasonable rules governing student conduct while on the field trip. Some suggestions to follow are: (1) always obtain the permission of parents before the trip; (2) secure enough qualified supervisors, even if it requires requesting additional aides or volunteers; and (3) investigate thoroughly any potential safety hazards present at the locations you plan to visit.

However, teachers need to be forewarned that while parent permission forms are a good idea, they do not serve as legal protection in cases where negligence may be claimed. Waivers signed by parents do not relieve teachers or aides of potential liability for children injured on a field trip. In other words, a school employee cannot escape the penalty for her own negligence even when a parent voluntarily waives his right to sue for damages.

Whenever possible you and your aide should take the proposed trip yourself before you take the entire class. Study every aspect of the place to be visited and write down as many thought-provoking questions as possible. Some teachers have their aides take photos or slides for orientation purposes in the class in order to prepare and familiarize the children prior to going on the actual field trip. This way they can get more meaningful impressions from their experiences. Other teachers send for any available printed materials so that the children can become familiar with the physical layout, the overall operation, scope, and procedures of the place to be visited. You and the aide should become as knowledgeable about the trip as possible so you can clarify the trip's purpose, procedures, rules, and regulations for the children.

The manner in which you and your aide conduct the follow-up activities after a field trip is almost as important as the trip itself. Your attitudes about the trip are quickly sensed and reflected by your class. By your enthusiasm and interest they know if you feel the excursion was a poor or an excellent one.

When the class returns to the school, your teacher aide can help the children to record their experiences in a variety of ways:

1. By composing oral or written reports
2. By writing poems
3. By drawing pictures about the trip
4. By creating narratives and stories

CORRIDOR DUTIES

You can often tell quite a bit about a school by the way the children behave in the corridors or hallways. Courtesy, citizenship, and cleanliness — these are only a few of the characteristics good teachers and schools try to make an integral part of the children's attitudes and actions in the classroom as well as in the remainder of the building. The corridors must be viewed as simply an extension of the classroom for teaching independence, good manners, and self-discipline. For these reasons and more, calm disposition, good eyesight, a sense of humor, and a great deal of patience are sensible and practical requirements for a good corridor monitor.

The aim of good discipline in the corridors, as well as in the classroom, is to help children adjust to the personal and social forces that are part of their experiences. First, the child must learn to adjust to himself as a growing and developing individual. Second, the youngster must adjust to the existing culture and institutions of which he is a part. Often, he will have to make a further adjustment by reconciling his home environment standards with those of the school. The problem of discipline today consists mainly of helping the child exercise self-restraint and develop acceptable inner controls.

It is up to teachers to make aides aware of the kind of problems they may encounter in the process of corridor supervision and to assist them in developing procedures for dealing effectively with certain behavioral characteristics. It would be wise for you to discuss the following types of behavioral problem patterns with your aide:

1. The child who conducts inappropriate activities in the corridor
2. The child who is impolite and inconsiderate
3. The child who runs in the corridor
4. The child who is late for class
5. The child who refuses to comply with an aide's request
6. The child who is destroying school property
7. The child who is eating candy inside the building
8. The child who is playing in the corridors
9. The child who does not have his teacher's permission to be in the corridor

At some time an aide may make a simple request of a child in the corridor only to discover that he refuses to obey. What should be done under these circumstances? The action to be taken will, of course, depend in large measure upon the nature of the request. Refusal to comply with a simple request, such as to stop loud talking, usually is associated with high emotional tension. The aide should be instructed not to argue with the child because continued argumentative dialogue only makes the situation worse. The aide should not make statements or threats which cannot be enforced or which give the child no face-saving alternative for subsequent behavior. Usually the aide can take the child by the hand and direct him toward that behavior which was requested. It is very important, however, that the aide's request be followed. Failure to comply should be subject to certain inevitable consequences. Unreasonable requests should be avoided. A reasonable request for one child may be unreasonable for another. Provide a cooling-off period to allow both the child and the aide to reduce their emotional levels and to become more objective about the circumstances. More often than not, the problem may then be more easily handled by both the aide and the child.

While it is difficult to list a series of "do's and don'ts" for teacher aides in discipline matters, some general guidelines may help improve an aide's ability to handle discipline problems. You might want to share the following list with your aide:

Do's

- Do try to get to know as many students personally as possible
- Do be consistent with students
- Do be fair with students
- Do reinforce desirable behavior
- Do reward whenever possible rather than punish
- Do try to be positive in your disciplinary approach

Don'ts

- Don't stereotype students
- Don't have favorites
- Don't accept poor behavior
- Don't ignore misbehavior
- Don't use negative punitive approaches too often
- Don't let personal emotions interfere with disciplinary actions

THE AIDE'S ROLE IN OTHER NONTEACHING FACILITIES

Children benefit directly from an aide being assigned to a classroom; however, aides can also indirectly provide a wide variety of supportive services outside the regular classroom. For instance, an aide assigned to the school psychologist or counselor may find herself doing some initial interviewing of students. She may also help children fill out forms and arrange for appointments with the psychologist or counselor. She may make home visits for the purpose of providing the counselor with information about the child's home environment. Aides who live in the community can be extremely useful in this capacity since the parents and students may be more relaxed with the aide than they would be with the counselor. The aide who is a resident of the community, particularly in lower socio-economic areas, will understand the subculture of the community much better. In this same context an aide may be able to "rap" with the child in the school situation, thereby preventing problems from arising in the first place by being on top of the situation. With an understanding and friendly reception, an encouraging word, and a sympathetic smile the counselor aide can help ease the nervous student or the anxious parent.

Likewise, an aide to the school nurse can provide numerous services to both the professional staff and to the children who attend the school. Such an aide can learn to keep health records, to give initial vision and hearing tests, and to help with the inoculation program. If the professional nurse is required to serve several schools, the aide will be able to keep the nurse informed as to which students require special care or attention during her next scheduled visit. In addition, the aide might provide services such as taking an ill child home, giving first aid treatment for minor cuts or bruises, or staying in the sick room with an ill child whose parents cannot be reached. However, it must be stressed that at no time is the aide to replace the nurse in her professional service to children. She has neither the training nor the experience to decide how seriously ill or hurt a child may be. The aide's role is always to free the nurse to perform more professional activities with the staff and with the children.

An aide assigned to the school office will soon find herself performing a wide variety of services for youngsters. Aides also can do odd jobs for the principal, help the secretary with any work overflow, and deal with the public. An aide serving in the office is really an all-purpose "Girl Friday." In dealing with the public the aide should always remember to be polite, should be careful not to commit her supervisors to a specific action, and should not guess about some information if she does not know for sure. She should always make notes concerning parent's visits or telephone calls and give the information promptly to the appropriate person.

Aides assigned to the school office need to be told that the school's primary task is to serve children. The students are the really important people who must be helped. Often the school secretary becomes overwhelmed with trying to solve the seemingly small problems which are considered to be really big to the youngsters involved. In this situation the office aide can be of real assistance. A quiet, reassuring voice which reflects concern and a willingness to help does much to show children that the school cares about their problems.

Finally, there is a trend towards extracurricular activities rapidly becoming an integral part of the established elementary school program. Many of these activities at the elementary level are similar to those at the secondary level. For example, there are choral groups, orchestras, bands, and special-interest clubs. Service organizations such as the safety patrol, library assistants, and the Junior Red Cross also continue to be important. Many elementary schools have school newspapers and a student council. As at the secondary level, selecting a sponsor for an activity is an important decision. Obviously, the sponsor should have enthusiasm and feel that the particular school activity to which she will devote her efforts is worthwhile. Aides can contribute immeasurably to the activity program by serving as cosponsors or as assistants to the sponsors. Aides selected for these purposes should possess a sincere interest in children and have an awareness of the problem areas likely to develop in the selected activity. The contributions of aides are many, but one of their most important contributions will be that of helping to create the positive attitude in the students that school is both meaningful and enjoyable.

SUMMARY

As we have seen in this chapter, teacher aides can be of

service in many areas outside the regular classroom. If they are effectively recruited and trained, aides can contribute to the overall successful operation of an elementary school. However, the experienced teacher should be well aware that such responsible tasks as playground, cafeteria, and corridor duty require not only patience but human relations expertise. It is up to you to provide your aide with the required proficiency she needs to successfully carry out the supervisory duties outside the classroom.

CHAPTER 8

THE VOLUNTEER AIDE

THE idea of volunteer services is far from new. For decades individuals have given their time and effort to all kinds of organizations — libraries, schools, welfare agencies, and hospitals. Usually their efforts were on a hit-or-miss basis, with individuals volunteering help as they found it was needed. Today, however, volunteer services have achieved a new sense of responsibility. Services no longer consist of only casual activities for people who have leisure time, but rather they represent an acceptance of the fact that community service is everyone's concern.

Although each school must develop its own volunteer program, there are a few general guidelines which may prove helpful. You, the teacher, with your principal and a group of parents, might discuss the topic of how and where volunteers could help. Make plans carefully and realistically. Second, establish lines of communication. Always be sincere in your request for assistance. List specific needs. Tell volunteer aides what is expected of them and how they can help. Third, match the job to the volunteer's talent. Try to place volunteers where their talents can be used to the best advantage. A parent who feels she would not be able to tutor a child may feel more comfortable assisting with games, art activities, and parties. Finally, remember that a volunteer aide program is a two-way process. As parents contribute to the school, the school in turn should make them feel wanted and needed. Express appreciation for the volunteers' help and be available to assist all of them to contribute their very best.

The use of volunteer aides is a very effective way of mobilizing resources in the community and of providing additional staff in all areas of an elementary school program. Volunteers also can help to build better community understanding of programs and can help stimulate wide-spread citizen support for improved services in various areas when local citizens are given the opportunity to be participants in school programs.

RECRUITING VOLUNTEERS

Just as teacher aide programs differ, so will the methods differ that are used to recruit volunteer workers. Regardless of the kind of program you plan, tailor your recruiting techniques to the situation in your classroom, in your school system, and in your community.

When you begin the process of recruiting volunteers, seek out men and women who love children and who are known to be reliable, friendly, and flexible. In selecting volunteers you should look for persons of diversified abilities, skills, and talents who are interested in serving the school. In general most teachers look for people with qualifications such as a "feeling" for children, experience in working with youngsters, a variety of outside interests, a neat appearance, good use of basic English, and good character.

There is an abundant untapped supply of talented persons in every city and town. Some of these are housewives whose professional occupations have been temporarily interrupted by the family's need for them to be full-time homemakers for a period of time. Others are retired persons with a wide variety of talent and experience. Many of these potential volunteers have degrees in the liberal arts; some probably have talent and training in such useful areas as art, music, design, or business education.

Your local high school can also provide another important source of volunteer personnel. Almost every high school has a group of talented students representing all areas of the curriculum who can assist elementary teachers for short periods of time. Performing some of the housekeeping and maintenance tasks as well as assisting with clerical and teaching chores provides valuable learning experiences for the student volunteer and much-needed assistance for the busy teacher.

One might ask where these talented people have been hiding. Some individuals are hesitant to offer their help for fear it will be resented or refused. Then, too, some are shy or feel that they have insufficient ability or training. Others have a natural reserve that prevents them from volunteering in an institution as revered as our public schools. Experience with volunteer help in other service agencies has shown that most of these inhibitions can be overcome through careful recruiting and appropriate orientation methods.

As an aid in recruiting, as well as in subsequent placement,

VOLUNTEER AIDE APPLICATION FORM

Name_____ Age_____

Home Address_____ Phone_____

Business Address_____ Phone_____

Education and Special Training_____
_____

Volunteer Experience_____
_____

What are your skills, talents, or hobbies?_____
_____

Do you play a musical instrument?_____ Which one?_____

Do you have a driver's license: Yes _____   No_____

Physical Limitations_____
_____

Referred by_____

Job Preference: Time Available:

1. _____   Monday_____

2. _____   Tuesday_____

3. _____   Wednesday_____

4. _____   Thursday_____

                                 Friday_____

                                 Saturday_____

_____
Signature of Volunteer

many school districts use a volunteer application form. Many of these forms ask for information such as educational background, work experience, volunteer experience, type of volunteer service preferred, and the days and hours they are available to serve regularly. A sample volunteer aide application form appears in this section.

Once an individual has made an application or expressed interest in becoming an aide, it would be wise to ask her to come to the school for an interview. This will give you an opportunity to observe the applicant's appearance, speech, and physical characteristics and to note any limitations. In addition, the interview will afford you the chance to assess her attitude and reason for wanting to serve as a volunteer aide. Always encourage the applicant to speak freely; also, refrain from monopolizing the conversation. Use this opportunity to give necessary information such as requirements for orientation and training, instructions concerning job requirements prior to selection, and a brief description of the aims of your volunteer program.

Keep in mind that your main objective during the interview is to obtain information about the volunteer. You might prepare a list of simple, informal questions that will accomplish the purpose of the interview. For instance, you might ask the applicant how she feels about the job and what her aspirations are concerning the volunteer effort. Be a good listener. Be alert to "clues" communicated by gestures, tone of voice, and facial expressions. Allow time for pauses and reflective moments during the interview. Remember, there are usually two volunteer applicants present at all interviews: the applicant as she really is and the applicant as she would like to appear.

Once a sufficient base of volunteer help has been established, personal contact and community discussion will aid in attracting additional volunteers. However, until such time as this is possible, general media contact can be helpful to let citizens know of your desire for volunteers. Announcements of meetings for all persons interested in giving their time and/or talent to help youngsters may be placed in the local newspaper or on radio or television. A handmade poster placed in a neighborhood grocery store window may also catch an eye or two. To be more selective about volunteers, contact local civic or social organizations which exhibit the qualities you desire in a volunteer aide. For example, male volunteers might be recruited through the local Lions Club or Jaycees.

As you recruit, keep in mind that a volunteer aide wants to feel some responsibility for the program — in its aim as well as in its accomplishments. Show that you realize her worth by giving her responsibility for important tasks, but do not lean upon her so heavily that she feels trapped. If she enjoys her volunteer work, she will respond by spreading her contagious enthusiasm to her friends and neighbors. That is the best method of recruiting more volunteers.

ORIENTATION ACTIVITIES

A successful volunteer aide program must include, in addition to careful planning and recruiting, a carefully designed and effectively executed orientation and training program. Unless volunteers know thoroughly their roles and responsibilities, the program will not come to full fruition.

The objective of orientation is to make the volunteer as comfortable as possible and to inform her of the goals of the school, taking care not to overwhelm her with too much, too fast. Orientation may be accomplished at least partially by means of an informal tour of the work setting accompanied by her introduction to permanent staff members and other volunteer workers. It is wise to provide volunteers with printed materials to inform them of the organization's aims and regulations. This material might include a brief handbook covering the following information:

- purpose of the organization
- names of key personnel
- volunteer expectations
- staff expectations of volunteers
- available assignments
- samples of records and forms

Assuming that the overall orientation program has been taken care of by the administrative staff, each teacher needs to direct her efforts toward orienting the volunteer to the specific tasks in her classroom. If a volunteer aide is not given a job description, she may enter into her work with the idea of doing what she pleases instead of what the teacher prefers. For example, the volunteer may desire to spend all of her time teaching the children a particular skill she possesses, but which is not included in the teacher's curriculum. She must be made fully aware of the curriculum requirements for the grade level in which she is going to work.

Before the volunteer's first day on the job, time should be set aside for the teacher and the volunteer to meet and discuss each of their roles in the classroom. The teacher should describe what she is trying to accomplish, her style of teaching, and her general method of operation. In addition, the teacher should find out what kinds of experiences the volunteer aide has had with children. Does she have specific outside interests or hobbies? What specialized training or education does she possess? If a volunteer's background is fully explored and then utilized, she is often able to contribute more to the class than the teacher in certain specific areas.

Within the classroom itself certain preparations should be made. For example, is there a place for the volunteer to hang her coat? Is there a place in the room where she can keep personal items as well as her work materials? A single empty drawer she can call her own provides a practical solution for keeping her materials together and also gives her a sense of "belonging." Will your volunteer need copies of the daily or weekly schedule? If so get them ready ahead of time. Let her borrow your copy if you cannot get an extra one. These procedures are particularly good ways of making her feel that she is part of the team, with the result that she will be eager to learn as much as she can about her school.

VOLUNTEER TRAINING

After the volunteer is placed, the type and amount of training required will depend upon the job to be done as well as the abilities and skills of the volunteer. Most volunteer aides feel that it is helpful to be provided with an adequate job description. This description should clarify the following:

- specific duties
- work relationships involved
- name of the person to whom the volunteer is immediately responsible
- legal status and ethical practices to be observed
- human aspect of working with children
- importance of regular attendance and punctuality in all tasks
- hours of service

The many factors involved in working with youngsters can be brought out during the volunteer's training period. For example, volunteers should be reminded of the fact that each home in the community sends a product of that particular background to school; this circumstance makes for many differences in the children within a single classroom. All of these differences and needs must be recognized and responded to by the volunteer. She can give the extra help sometimes needed for a child to reach his potential. Quite often, a youngster will work especially hard to gain respect from a new adult in his life. Also, the child is usually impressed that there is someone who cares enough about him to work for free.

Volunteers, like teacher aides, must be given the opportunity to continue to learn. Aides are seldom satisfied that they know all the answers. As paraprofessionals they are continually striving to learn more about their job and to develop new skills. So, too, must the volunteer be given an opportunity to grow. Volunteers should, for example, be invited from time to time to attend regular faculty meetings so that they can learn more about how their school operates. If the professional staff is involved in an in-service program, volunteer aides should be invited to attend. When regular full-time aides receive materials which are related to their function and role, the same materials should be distributed to the volunteer aides as well.

A volunteer can also learn to be more effective by visiting other classrooms within the building. Perhaps she could benefit by learning more about a special project being conducted by a teacher upstairs or by observing a staff member in another building who is doing something different in group work. Since it is good experience for other teachers to see these innovations, it is also good experience for volunteer aides.

Likewise, an opportunity for a volunteer to talk with her teacher in terms of "How am I progressing?" or "How else can I assist you?" can be a valuable training experience. Obviously, in the final analysis, it will be the teacher who will bear the greatest share of responsibility for helping the volunteer to improve her skills. A volunteer who desires to be of service will welcome the opportunity to discuss with her supervising teacher how she can improve her job skills.

Ultimately, the effectiveness of any volunteer training effort can be measured by the morale of the individuals involved in the program. It is important that teachers in leadership roles possess the necessary level of sensitivity to determine the state of a volunteer's morale. Good morale is usually present when individuals (1) satisfy their need to participate, express their feelings, and receive recognition; (2) manifest the qualities of determination, confidence, and enthusiasm; and (3) feel that they are moving in a direction where they can attain their goals.

Finally, it should be remembered that volunteer aides are not employed for the purpose of making the teacher's job easier. They are employed to assist in improving the educational environment of children. The youngsters in the classroom are intended to be the chief beneficiaries. If you are guided by this important consideration, you should have little difficulty in making most of the decisions that are essential in regard to the training and utilization of volunteer aides.

WORKING WITH A VOLUNTEER

If teachers are required to carefully analyze the teaching situation and determine the best possible use of volunteer aides, chances are much better that the program will be successful. Teachers who plan worthwhile activities for volunteers on the basis of an analysis of student needs will be able to make their instructional programs work much more effectively. As a result, there will be fewer chances for disappointment or failure since each of the selected activities will have been carefully planned by the staff member utilizing the volunteer.

However, before any aide can be of service to children she must be fully integrated into the classroom routine. You might choose to begin this process by introducing the students to the new volunteer helper. Depending on the kinds of activities you have planned for her first day, you might elect to let her mingle with and observe the students as they are engaged in their regular classroom work. Be sure to take a few minutes of your time to explain to the new aide how your daily routine is conducted. If possible give her a copy of your classroom activity schedule. Additional time spent now will probably be repaid time and again in the days ahead as the volunteer becomes more proficient at her job.

Some time after the volunteer aide appears on the scene you will need to define to your class her position in terms of her role and authority. This might be accomplished best by giving her an opportunity to use some authority. If this is done successfully, the children will observe your support and respect for the volunteer and be much more willing to accept her as someone who is also in charge.

If a volunteer aide "goofs" in the classroom, it will be your responsibility to get her off the spot as gracefully as possible. Some teachers find that the use of humor in such situations makes the entire experience less traumatic for both the volunteer and the youngsters. Nevertheless, if too many mistakes appear, it may well be a result of insufficient planning or poor communication between the partners.

In addition, there are a number of things the volunteer aide must know before she can begin to function properly. Some questions that have been developed in regard to regular full-time instructional aides have their parallel in the utilization of volunteers. These are as follows:

1. What are the volunteer's special and regular duties?
2. With whom should the volunteer discuss a matter of school policy?
3. Who will have priority in regard to use of the volunteer's time?
4. What are the most important rules and regulations with which the volunteer should be familiar?
5. With what equipment will the volunteer most likely be expected to work?
6. With what supplies will the volunteer be expected to work?
7. Where are the special facilities with which the volunteer should become familiar?

Experience has shown that it takes several weeks in most cases before volunteers and teachers begin to function as a true educational team. When this happy circumstance does begin to occur in the classroom, all the time and effort spent on orientation and training will begin to pay off for the teacher. A good team relationship can and must be developed.

MAKING A RESOURCE-PERSON FILE

Many enrichment activities that would be both pertinent and relevant for elementary school children just cannot be carried out because the teacher has neither the time nor talent for such projects. On the other hand, many parents and other lay persons have special abilities a teacher can use in her classroom. Carpentry is a good example. Girls as well as boys need to learn how to use a hammer and saw. A parent who is proficient in carpentry can be a welcome asset in the classroom. Or, an individual with a knack for stitchery can supervise this type of activity. Remember, resource persons live just around the corner from every school.

Whom could you invite? Invite just about anyone you feel has something to share. One ingenious teacher invited a mother she knew who was an especially good cook. The mother came one morning each week to a fourth grade class-

room to assist the teacher in some very enjoyable cooking projects. Another teacher had a parent who filmed the youngsters
during a dramatics session and on a field trip. Then she
showed the films, giving the children much delight in seeing
themselves in remembered situations.

Even if your school district is small and you have no system-
wide resource department or staff, you can run your own community resource program — probably much more easily than
you think. However, most parents and other individuals, although interested, are busy. They tend to shy away from any
overstructured organization. For that reason one of the most
effective methods of getting them involved is to take into consideration their busy schedules and avoid a formal type of organizational structure. Formal committees and almost endless
meetings are really unnecessary.

Instead, make it a point to always be on the alert for possible
resource people within your own community. Some teachers
make it a regular practice to search the local newspaper for
interesting personalities or individuals with special talents.
Others seek out individuals whom they meet in their regular
work and social life. A single telephone call will usually determine the availability of the person as a possible resource for
some future classroom activity. More often than not, the individual will be flattered that you have sought him out to make a
presentation to the youngsters in your class.

The wise teacher, however, will usually carry the process one
step further by developing a resource-person file. She might
choose to keep it simple by merely writing the information
(name, address, telephone number, resource area, etc.) on an
index card. Or, she may decide to develop a loose-leaf notebook
containing information sheets about all potential volunteers,
listed according to subject specialty. Then, for example, if she
desires a speaker on forestry to supplement the science curriculum, she simply consults the resource notebook for volunteers
qualified to speak on the subject.

When you form the habit of looking for resource people to
bring to your classroom, you often latch on to some really
interesting individuals with exciting topics. Nevertheless, when

a resource person is brought into the classroom, his visit must be carefully planned. A teacher should use the following principles as a guide:

- The speaker must be able to effectively communicate with your age group.
- The topic must meet the needs of the class.
- The contribution must be worthwhile.
- The speaker must be given a time limit.
- The youngsters should write thank-you letters.

USING COMMUNITY ASSETS

Closely allied to the use of individual volunteers in the classroom is the utilization of community resources. Neighborhood and community groups are a veritable treasure of resources for your classroom. When you let them know of your interest, service clubs, church groups, and other community agencies will often volunteer their help.

Executives of more and more commercial establishments are demonstrating their feeling that as community leaders they should work to enrich the life of the community they serve. This point of view is particularly prevalent among newspaper owners, many of whom sponsor a variety of community service events. Typical of these programs are the following:

- *Spelling Bees.* Locally sponsored spelling bees produce winners who continue their competition and progress as far as their talent and luck will take them. Conceivably, they could enter and win the National Spelling Bee title in Washington, D.C.
- *Science Fairs.* Student projects are rewarded with cash prizes, certificates, and scholarships, with the eventual possibility of a free trip to the national science fair.
- *Scholastic Writing and Scholastic Art Awards.* Associated nationally with *Scholastic Magazine*, the contests enable elementary school youngsters not only to win at the local level but to compete nationally.

But what if these community projects are not available in

your locality? One possible answer is to encourage your local newspaper and other businesses to develop and sponsor these or similar projects. Most businessmen are aware of their community service responsibilities and will react positively to a well-thought out program which benefits youngsters.

When you inaugurate your program, there are a few basic guidelines to follow. First of all, the projected program must be outlined in depth, including what facilities will be required, who will be directly and indirectly involved, how many individuals will be needed to conduct the program, and, of course, how much money the program will cost.

The next step is to take it to the proposed sponsor. In most large cities newspapers and other businesses have public relations departments. In smaller communities ask to see the general manager of the particular commercial establishment. Ideally, these are the people with whom to start the discussion since ultimately they will be the ones to either approve or reject the project. The program should be explained in detail, orally and in writing. The sponsor's participation in the program, down to the last detail, should be outlined, including what the final costs will be. The public relations advantage to that particular sponsor should be vividly illustrated, including the information such as how many student homes the particular project will touch or influence.

Community industries can be used to everyone's advantage as sponsors of projects that encourage and develop more fully the student's thirst for knowledge. With resources in most communities widening daily, effective teaching and learning should include all available community resources in order to relate the outside world to the world of your classroom.

SUMMARY

The utilization of volunteer aides in the classroom brings them in closer contact with the professional staff. This interaction and exchange of ideas and information helps both the teachers and volunteers in their efforts to educate youngsters to become functional members of society. Education then becomes truly a school-community enterprise.

The community benefits because there is a wider dissemination of school information throughout the community. People living in the community are more completely and correctly informed about your educational program; also, they can communicate with other citizens who never visit the school except casually for a PTA meeting or a student assembly.

In addition, individuals benefit because they see firsthand what the school is trying to accomplish. They also begin to see the school's program and role in terms of other people's interests, experiences, and values as well as their own. Through this active participation, volunteers are better able to view the interrelated education roles of the school and the community.

CHAPTER 9

EVALUATING YOUR TEACHER AIDE

THE evaluation of teacher aides is often looked upon by the classroom teacher as a necessary evil, yet it can be a valuable tool in the process of improving instruction. Remember, every teacher aide wants to succeed, just as every teacher does. Most aides will welcome evaluation if it promises to help them become more effective members of the teaching team. Therefore, teacher aide appraisal should be continuous rather than just periodic. It should be accompanied by, and followed with, helpful supervision.

In order to conduct a successful evaluation program the classroom teacher must accept responsibility for acquainting the aide with what is expected of her and what appraisal techniques are to be utilized. Aides should be encouraged to think in positive terms of the evaluation process and consider it a constructive source of help. Also, the teacher must avoid giving the impression that the evaluation instrument will be regarded as the final verdict on the teacher aide's work or worth.

Most teachers agree that the very fact that aides know their performance is being observed and recorded tends to keep them on their toes. This does not imply that aides will consistently fail to put forth maximum effort unless they are under continual surveillance. Neither does it mean that classroom aides have an undue need for constant praise and encouragement in order to perform at peak efficiency. Rather, aides are like all the rest of us — they perform much better when they know that their work is understood and appreciated by their supervisors.

One of the most important benefits of evaluation is that it encourages teachers to do more analytical and constructive thinking about the performance of aides. In the process it often forces the teacher herself to recognize and face up to some of her own prejudices and biases. It should also help her to question whether or not any of her feelings about the aide may be without sufficient foundation or are unreasonable. The performance-appraisal process should help teachers to be more specific about their aide's strong and weak points and help them to perceive that each aide is different. Understand that the appraisal process involves the evaluation not only of the aide's work, but also of your own performance.

Finally, if we examine teacher aide evaluation programs that seem to succeed as well as those that seem to fail, certain basic patterns begin to appear. Although it is unlikely that we can pinpoint all or even a majority of the elements that make up a successful program, certain specific characteristics and principles appear to be essential. These include the following:

1. Aides as well as teachers and principals need to be actively involved in developing the evaluation procedures.
2. A long period of planning, study, and preparation usually precedes the initiation of the evaluation process.
3. The primary purpose of the evaluation program is to improve instruction and to help aides succeed.
4. Evaluation is always based on firsthand observation of the teacher aide's classroom performance.
5. Evaluations are recorded on a checklist or other instrument that has been developed cooperatively with the aides.
6. The evaluation process itself is evaluated periodically and changed whenever improvement is possible.

SELECTING THE CRITERIA FOR EVALUATION

More often than not, the effectiveness of an evaluation program will depend to a great extent upon the criteria selected. Therefore, early in the developmental stages of a teacher aide evaluation program the persons involved in the planning process must decide how the aide is to be evaluated. In other words what criteria will be utilized in appraising her work?

If the purpose of the evaluation process is primarily to improve instruction and to upgrade the existing aide corps, the teacher is probably justified in placing more emphasis on objectives relating to performance and student progress than on personality traits. Presumably you can expect the aide to change her work procedures and methods more easily and readily than her attitudes and basic disposition. However, an evaluator can measure only those things she can see with a fair amount of objectivity. Thus, do not seek to ask how good an aide is, but, rather, ask what she is doing. How well does she follow instructions? Does she get along well with the students? Does she perform routine tasks efficiently? By using this approach you take the pressure off the aide as an individual.

Characteristically, the teacher aide evaluation should include the following major categories:

RELATIONSHIPS WITH CHILDREN. Items should include such criteria as friendliness, helpfulness, fairness, liking for children, sympathy, patience, and skill in resolving conflicts.

RELATIONSHIPS WITH THE CLASSROOM TEACHER. Items should include such criteria as willingness to accept directions, dependability in meeting commitments and assignments, initiative and alertness in meeting teacher needs, punctuality, and efficient use of time and materials.

PERSONAL APPEARANCE AND ATTITUDES. Items here should be concerned with attendance, temperament, dress, grooming, courtesy, and willingness to give time and effort to the job.

SCHOOL-COMMUNITY RELATIONS. Items could include such areas as using discretion in discussing school and community matters, knowledge and use of proper channels of communication, and awareness of school policies and routines.

It might be suggested that in developing criteria for evaluating teacher aides we substitute a new focus on aide improvement for the old focus on aide shortcomings. Beginning and ending with the teacher aide's self-appraisal, the assessment process should concentrate on agreed-upon areas for improvement. The whole procedure should be based on the assumption that the aide will improve if given the proper encouragement and help she needs to do so. In such an atmosphere of faith and trust, improvement is far more likely to occur than in an atmosphere of fear and coercion fostered by the more conventional approaches to evaluation.

USING EVALUATION INSTRUMENTS

In an attempt to make evaluation more objective, many different kinds of evaluation instruments have been developed. Almost all of these are paper-and-pencil devices. Generally these instruments contain a list of statements which describe traits, activities, and performances that have been determined to be essential to effective aide behavior. Each item on the list is followed by a scale, with grades ranging from poor to superior, by which the teacher or supervisor indicates his or her own judgment of how well the teacher aide rates on the particular item. When using these forced-choice instruments, the evaluator focuses his or her attention on relevant items; that is, he or she does so if the selected items are truly descriptive of a good teacher aide.

When selecting an instrument to measure aide performance based on the areas that affect it, bear in mind that the nature of what is to be evaluated should determine the type of instrument that should be used. One instrument, for example, may be excellent for evaluating the personality traits of an aide but will be of little value in appraising her classroom performance. Therefore, determine which aspects of aide behavior need to be measured and then attempt to describe the necessary characteristics of an instrument appropriate for measuring them.

For instance, one widely used instrument for obtaining information about teacher aide performance is the inventory. It attempts to list as many relevant statements as possible about teacher aide performance. The evaluator then judges the extent and frequency of which these statements apply to the aide under observation. Such inventories are valuable in directing attention to problem areas. They also may indicate the frequency of such behavior.

Checklists are adaptations of inventories. They are designed for ease of marking and can be constructed in such a way as to measure the presence or absence of a particular trait, condition, or process. As used in teacher aide evaluations, the checklist usually consists of a list of traits or skills against which the evaluator checks those traits or skills manifested by the aide under consideration. In most cases, the checklist can be employed either by the aide herself as she reacts to various statements or by the classroom teacher as she checks observed behavior on the part of the teacher aide.

Another technique often used to measure and record aide performance is the rating scale. This device usually contains a list of phrases or sentences which describe varying degrees of a behavior, trait, or process. The list is arranged in order from low proficiency to high. The evaluator then selects the statement that in his or her opinion best describes the individual being rated.

However, in a practical school situation do not expect that teacher aide evaluations can be conducted as rigorously or as scientifically as in formal research studies. The evaluation instrument may not be as precise, and controls cannot be applied as strictly. Try, nevertheless, to have some general knowledge of

SAMPLE I

TEACHER AIDE EVALUATION INVENTORY

Name_____ School_____ Date_____

	Excellent	Above Average	Average	Below Average	Unsatisfactory
General Appearance					
Personal Characteristics					
Attitude Toward Job					
Attitude Toward Children					
Ability to Help and Work with Teacher					
Enthusiasm					
Punctuality and Attendance					
Health					
Speech					
Clerical Skills					
Overall Evaluation of Aide					

Do you recommend the aide for reemployment in your classroom? Yes_____ No_____

_____
Evaluator

SAMPLE II

TEACHER AIDE EVALUATION RATING SCALE

Name_____ Date_____

School_____ Assigned Area_____

RATING: Poor to Superior

	Poor								Superior	
	1	2	3	4	5	6	7	8	9	10
Interest & Enthusiasm										
Personality										
Appearance										
Reliability										
Ethics										
Adaptability										
Effectiveness										
Ability										
Initiative										
Emotional Stability										

Please add any comments which would contribute to the evaluation:

_____

_____

What efforts and improvements have been made by the aide in her performance?_____

_____

_____

Do you recommend the aide for reemployment?   Yes _____   No_____

Signatures:

Teacher_____ Aide_____

the procedures for evaluating aides and know what can be achieved under ideal conditions.

A variety of teacher aide evaluation forms have been provided in this chapter. However, you should be aware of the benefits to be derived from working cooperatively with your aide in order to design your own evaluation instrument, one which, it would be hoped, more nearly meets the needs of your own particular classroom and/or school.

SAMPLE III

TEACHER AIDE EVALUATION CHECKLIST

Aide's Name_____ Date _____
School_____ Grade Level _____
Directions: On the basis of the items listed below, please rate your teacher aide according to the following scale:

4   3   2   1

Highest   Lowest

_____ 1. Shows interest and enthusiasm in her work.
_____ 2. Accepts changes in assignments willingly.
_____ 3. Is punctual in meeting commitments.
_____ 4. Follows instructions and directions.
_____ 5. Shows respect for rights, feelings, and opinions of others.
_____ 6. Interacts positively with students.
_____ 7. Accepts individual differences in students.
_____ 8. Shows resourcefulness in helping to provide enrichment experiences for students.
_____ 9. Is competent in reinforcement of basic learning skills.
_____10. Has a minimum of distracting and irritating mannerisms.
_____11. Asks for suggestions and assistance.
_____12. Is alert and displays vitality most of the time.
_____13. Is aware of the basic tenets of child development.
_____14. Is able to work with small groups for instructional purposes.
_____15. Shows concern for children's health and safety.
_____16. Has a friendly working relationship with other teacher aides.
_____17. Demonstrates loyalty to the teacher and the school.
_____18. Circulates among students on the playground.
_____19. Gives willingly of time and special talents.
_____20. Helps students use class time effectively.
_____21. Reacts to emergency situations calmly.
_____22. Shows fairness in dealing with children.
_____23. Displays an even temper most of the time.
_____24. Makes necessary preparations for assigned responsibilities.
_____25. Is acquainted with and follows school routine and district policies.
_____26. Is cheerful and pleasant most of the time.
_____27. Uses discretion in discussing school matters.

_____28. Does extra work.

_____29. Knows when and how to refer problems to the proper authorities.

_____30. Is well groomed and appropriately dressed.

_____31. Has good physical health.

_____32. Shows evidence of constructive professional growth.

_____33. Supervises small group activities.

_____34. Obtains and operates AV equipment and materials effectively.

_____35. Assumes some supervisory responsibilities during special classes.

_____36. Assists in administering tests under the teacher's supervision.

_____37. Assumes an active role in planning goals and instructional activities with the teacher.

_____38. Avoids criticism of the children, teacher, and the school.

_____39. Assists with keeping the room neat and orderly.

_____40. Arranges and supervises indoor games on rainy days.

_____41. Instructs children on proper use and safety of tools.

_____42. Emphasizes courtesy and good manners.

UTILIZING SELF-EVALUATION TECHNIQUES

As indicated before, self-evaluation or self-appraisal can be an effective instrument for teacher aide evaluation. It has not, however, been completely accepted by many educational authorities. They usually point out that many aides, particularly those who are marginal or insecure, tend to overrate themselves. Each tends to think she is doing as well as she can under the circumstances. Few aides are able to be objective in assessing their own performance; consequently, their self-evaluations are both inaccurate and unreliable.

Nevertheless, teachers sometimes point out that the inadequacies of self-evaluation are not necessarily basic weaknesses in the technique but result from either misuse of the technique or the failure to understand the basic purposes of teacher aide evaluation. If evaluation is regarded, as it should be, as a means of improving performance rather than as a mere rating system, then self-appraisal becomes an important part of the total evaluation process.

In fact, there are some important reasons why self-evaluation techniques should be included in the assessment process:

1. When self-evaluation is utilized, the teacher aide shares with her teacher the responsibility for improving her performance.

2. Teacher aides, particularly those aspiring to enhance their own professional status, regard self-evaluation as the most acceptable method for evaluating performance.
3. Self-evaluation should be the ultimate goal of any evaluation program that seeks to promote better classroom performance. The best and only effective motive for change is one that comes from within.

If a teacher aide is to grow and improve her services to children, she must want to change. She must develop her own expectations and standards of satisfactory and superior performance. With such insights she can judge how closely her actual performance measures up to her expectations of herself. Unless aides are helped to recognize their own strengths and weaknesses, evaluation will have little permanent influence on the classroom teaching and learning situation.

But remember, effective use of self-appraisal methods in a teacher aide evaluation program requires careful planning. First of all, the classroom teacher must establish a proper climate for effective self-evaluation. If aides are to be proficient in evaluating themselves, they must have an opportunity to have a voice in the development of any checklist or instrument devised for that purpose. Secondly, teacher aides must be prepared for self-evaluation. This process should be a continual one throughout the school year. The aide should be assisted to see herself objectively at work so she can gain insight into her capabilities in the areas in which change is necessary if she is to improve. Finally, when the aide is called upon to appraise herself — whether on a formal evaluation checklist or otherwise — be sure that she understands the relationship of her evaluation to classroom performance and that she does not view appraisal as simply a rating device.

Deciding who should ultimately evaluate an aide should depend on the needs of the particular school system as well as the overall abilities of its staff. No standard rule of thumb can be established for this task. Successful teacher aide evaluation programs can be found in which the principal, a supervisor, the classroom teacher, or the aides themselves do the evaluating. The person who conducts the evaluation does not seem to be as important to the success or failure of the program as do these two aspects: (1) responsibility must be definite, and aides and all other personnel involved must know exactly where their responsibilities lie; and (2) the person evaluating must be reasonably competent.

If your principal or you decide to undertake a self-evaluation approach, the sample forms which appear in this section should aid you in the development of a satisfactory checklist or other type of appraisal instrument.

SAMPLE I

TEACHER AIDE SELF-EVALUATION CHECKLIST

Teacher Aide's Name _____

School _____   Teacher's Name _____   Date _____

Directions: Check the appropriate column

	Always	Usually	Rarely
1. Do I cooperate with the classroom teacher?			
2. Am I aware of the importance of the responsibilities assigned?			
3. Do I follow the directions given by the teacher?			
4. Do I follow through with lessons initiated by the teacher?			
5. Do I plan for the activity that I have been assigned?			
6. Do I check my completed assignments for mistakes and errors?			
7. Am I prompt in carrying out the duties assigned to me?			
8. Am I dependable and reliable?			
9. Do I exhibit initiative?			
10. Do I accept criticism?			
11. Do I avoid criticism of the children, the teacher, and the school?			
12. Do I try to develop a friendly attitude toward all of my co-workers?			

13. Do I strive to do my best at all times and take advantage of every opportunity?														
14. Is my handwriting, both manuscript and cursive, improving?														
15. Am I trying to improve my speech patterns?														
16. Do I operate audiovisual equipment efficiently?														
17. Am I aware of differences among students?														
18. Do children respond positively to me?														
19. Do children come to me for advice voluntarily?														
20. Am I conscious of each student's potentials and needs?														
21. Do I treat children fairly?														
22. Am I able to secure the cooperation of the students?														
23. Do I listen to the children?														
24. Am I a good listener?														
25. Am I courteous at all times?														
26. Do I present a favorable image of the school to the public?														
27. Do I show evidence of professional growth?														
28. Are my dress and appearance appropriate?														
29. Do I exhibit self-control?														
30. Am I in good health?														
31. Do I follow proper channels in communications and other activities?														
32. Do I evaluate myself at intervals?														
33. Do I enjoy my work?														

SAMPLE II

HOW DO I RATE AS A TEACHER AIDE?

Name _____ Date _____

School _____ Teacher _____

Key: Indicate A for excellent
              B for very good
              C for passable
              D for poor, needs improvement

____ 1. Change where necessary to meet new and different circumstances.

____ 2. Am punctual in arrival, turning in reports and assignments, and in meeting commitments.

____ 3. Follow instructions and directions.

____ 4. Show respect for rights, feelings, and opinions of others.

____ 5. Am aware of each student's interests.

____ 6. Am mindful of individual differences, abilities, and needs.

____ 7. Give all students equal opportunities and equal attention.

____ 8. Encourage students to assist each other.

____ 9. Avoid judging students by adult standards.

____10. Accept worthwhile suggestions.

____11. Am aware of teacher's needs and problems and find opportunities to give assistance.

____12. Have a minimum of distracting and irritating mannerisms.

____13. Comply with requests without additional reminding.

____14. Attempt to resolve conflicts on the playground and in the classroom.

____15. Show fairness in dealing with students.

____16. Willing to put in essential time and effort.

____17. Perform routine tasks efficiently.

____18. Interact positively with the students.

____19. Take charge of one group of students while the teacher works with another group.

____20. Contribute daily to planning long-range program for the students.

____21. Assist the students in learning proper social habits, including being polite to others.

____22. Assist students in library work.

____23. Help students learn proper use of tools and equipment.

____24. Help to keep the classroom neat and attractive.

____25. Show resourcefulness in helping provide enrichment experiences for students.

____26. Follow proper channels in communications and other activities.

____27. Help students use class time effectively.

____28. Make necessary preparation for assigned responsibilities.

____29. Show sympathy toward and understanding of children with problems.

____30. Am willing to admit error or lack of knowledge about a particular area.

____31. Participate in school activities.

____32. Participate in appropriate community activities.

____33. Am appropriately dressed for assigned duties.

____34. Use discretion when speaking of school or colleagues.

____35. Show willingness to share ideas and techniques.

____36. Contribute constructively to committee work.

____37. Use acceptable English in a clear and pleasant voice.

____38. Have good physical health.

____39. Show evidence of professional growth.

VALUE OF ANECDOTAL RECORDS

In assessing and evaluating teacher aide performance, anecdotal records can be an invaluable adjunct to observation. They offer the obvious advantage of being written records of behavior. Time, somehow, seems to have a way of clouding and confusing the true picture even when seen by the most skilled observer who, after all, may inject his own biases into his observations.

When anecdotal records are maintained over a period of time, they begin to show clear patterns of aide behavior and characteristic responses to problem situations. They can also record progress, change, and improvement as the teacher aide gains experience and insight. It is important that the teacher feel free to give a true picture of the aide as she sees her in order to facilitate evaluation.

The following suggestions may be useful in helping you to record and interpret anecdotal records on teacher aides:

1. The form used for recording anecdotes should be short and informal. Basically it should contain the name, date, situation or setting, description of behavior, and the observer's name.
2. Brief sentences are advisable, with a minimum of adverbs and adjectives.
3. Both strengths and weaknesses should be reported.
4. Since behavior is often conditioned by the situation or environment in which it occurs, it is advisable to record the setting.
5. Record the anecdote as soon as possible after the event.

Anecdotal records then are facts recorded as objectively as we can make them; they are not interpretations. They should contain details regarding specific situations. The date, the situation, a brief description of the behavior, possible explanations, and the recorder's signature constitute one entry. This record is often kept for several years in order to better establish patterns of behavior. Thus, such records may be used as an aid in gaining new insights into a teacher aide's development — a comparison between present behavior and that previously recorded — to determine consistent characteristics as well as new growth. The records can often be used as a basis for a cooperative conference with the teacher aide herself.

THE POSTEVALUATION CONFERENCE

For the purposes of improving the teacher aide's classroom performance, the most significant phase of the entire evaluation process may well be the postevaluation conference between the aide and her immediate supervisor. One main purpose of this conference is to inform the aide as to what she has achieved in terms of what she was expected to achieve. Equally important, the conference should be expected to lead to concrete suggestions and recommendations for improving performance where it has been weak and for the further development of strengths where performance has been satisfactory.

Both the teacher and the aide should prepare for the evaluation conference by thoroughly reviewing any evaluation forms that may have been utilized. It is further recommended that ample and uninterrupted time be allowed for the conference. Achieving this may necessitate conducting the conference in a private setting within the school. During the conference you should try to put the aide at ease and encourage her to express her views as to why her performance was above, on, or below an expected level of achievement. Usually the evaluation form itself will serve as the agenda. During some conferences, however, there may be only a general discussion concerning performance, usually to stress a particular point.

In addition, the postevaluation conference is an ideal time for clearing up any grievances that either you or your teacher aide may have. Disagreements concerning some phase of the aide's performance can be discussed and more than likely be resolved. Differing viewpoints and ideas can also be reconciled through discussion. Whenever the postevaluation conference is executed effectively, it provides an opportunity for you to motivate your aide to improve her classroom performance.

A teacher is more likely to conduct a successful postevaluation conference when she is well prepared in attitude as well as intellectually. Therefore:

1. Be objective in appraising the performance of the teacher aide. Evaluate results achieved against results expected in "specific observable terms."
2. Keep alert for important factors within the classroom which give insight into the teacher aide's on-the-job performance.
3. Develop an effective way of recording the aide's actions, so that this can be used as a gauge for analysis and evaluation.
4. When analyzing the aide's performance, base your judgments on observations which are derived from watching, listening, and inquiring for the purpose of getting complete and accurate information.
5. The teacher should evaluate the performance not only of the aide, but also of herself, especially in terms of how well the aide is being assisted in meeting her own objectives.

Further, the teacher should encourage the aide to do most of the talking at the conference. It is the teacher aide's development with which the teacher should be concerned; therefore, the teacher should provide the impetus that motivates the aide to speak freely. The teacher must remember that her primary task is to guide and assist the aide in achieving her objectives.

When the postevaluation conference has terminated, the wise teacher should carefully review her notes and mentally check through the conference to assess her own effectiveness as a supervisor. In this process she should review what went "wrong" and what went "right," reflecting on what she can do in the next conference to improve her own effectiveness. Some teachers find it helpful to write a self-evaluation report and periodically refer to this report to gauge the progress made in becoming a more efficient conferee.

EVALUATION AND MORALE

Evaluation cannot achieve its intended purpose unless it is cooperatively approached by both the teacher and aide. It would seem therefore that the teacher's main task is to determine ways of stimulating aide performance. Attempting to fit her methods and techniques to the teacher aide's personality and encouraging self-evaluation with stress on analyzing strengths and weaknesses are of utmost importance.

It must be recognized that teacher aide evaluation is a very potent process. If evaluations are incorrectly handled, they can damage staff morale. Although a teacher cannot control the situation entirely, she can do much to promote good morale. Cooperative planning of a beneficial evaluation program offers opportunities for better mutual understanding and stronger relationships.

The process of motivating aides does not necessitate direct stimulation from them to achieve objectives effectively; rather, of greater importance is the process of removing conditions which make aides dissatisfied with their performances. When an aide believes in and understands what must be achieved, she will exert the required effort to perform well on the job. Also, the teacher must therefore recognize that the best way to get a teacher aide to perform efficiently is to make her want to do it — to help her to become motivated.

All of us have our own zones of acceptable performance requirements. These psychological zones consist of areas of responsibility in which we feel obligated to produce satisfactory results according to the expectations we have set for ourselves. Job requirements that we feel fall within this so-called zone will be achieved with few problems. However, performance requirements which we feel fall outside of this zone will probably be achieved carelessly. The real role of the teacher as a motivator is to enlarge this psychological zone to encompass a greater area of personal involvement. The successful achievement of this goal will be reflected in an aide's attitude and behavior.

Morale, high and low, is contagious; in time it permeates the entire staff and can be influential in determining the quality of classroom instruction. Certainly, without high morale the teacher aide cannot operate with maximum effectiveness.

SUMMARY

Many more teacher aide appraisal programs have failed than have succeeded. It is apparent that the two most important characteristics of a successful program are (1) both the aide and the supervising teacher are actively involved in developing the evaluation plan, and (2) the purpose of the evaluation is essentially to improve the quality of instruction and to assist the aide in improving her classroom skills. As long as aides are evaluated by their supervisors in a formal on-going program, they have a right to expect that the evaluation will be conducted as fairly and objectively as possible. In fact unless teacher aide evaluations are to be conducted carefully and effectively, they should not be initiated in the first place. Experience indicates, however, that if an appraisal program is developed with care, instituted democratically, and administered fairly, it has great potential for improving teacher aide performance.

Selecting the criteria for the measurement of teacher aide effectiveness is probably the most important and yet the most difficult task in the development of an appraisal program. Typically, teacher aide evaluation includes such categories as the aide's relationship with the children and the classroom teacher, personal appearance and attitudes, and school-community relations. Criteria for evaluation, then, must clearly communicate the intended educational outcomes as well as the teacher aide's performance.

Finally, the evaluation tool selected for obtaining information about the teacher aide should be appropriate. Bear in mind that the nature and quality of what is to be measured should determine the type of evaluation instrument that is ultimately selected. However, it has been suggested that administrators and teachers work cooperatively with their aides in developing an instrument which meets their own particular needs.

SELECTED BIBLIOGRAPHY

Alexander, Kern. "What Teacher Aides Can — and Cannot — Do," *Nation's Schools*, *83*:23-25, August, 1968.

Association for Childhood Education. *Aides to Teachers and Children.* Washington, D.C.: The Association, 1968.

Bowman, Garda W. *New Careers and Roles in the American School.* New York: Bank Street College, 1968.

Branick, John H. "How to Train and Use Teacher Aides," *Phi Delta Kappan*, *48*:61, October, 1966.

Brighton, Howard. *Handbook for Teacher Aides.* Midland, Michigan: Pendell, 1972.

Brotherson, Mary Lou. *Teacher Aide Handbook: A Guide for New Careers in Education.* Danville, Ill.: Interstate, 1971.

Coppock, Nan and Templeton, Ian. *Paraprofessionals: School Leadership Digest.* Washington D.C.: National Association of Elementary School Principals, 1974.

Cull, John C. and Hardy, Richard E. *Volunteerism: An Emerging Profession.* Springfield, Ill.: Charles C Thomas Publisher, 1974.

Denemark, George W. "The Teacher and His Staff," *National Education Association Journal*, *87*:17-19, December, 1966.

Esbensen, Thorwald. "Should Teacher Aides Be More Than Clerks," *Phi Delta Kappan*, *47*:237, January, 1966.

Filmer, Thompson H. "Professional Reading Activities for Paraprofessionals," *Reading Teacher*, *26*:806-809, May, 1973.

Horburger, M. Jane. *So You Have An Aide.* Wilmington, Del.: Wilmington Public Schools, 1971.

Howe, Robert S. *The Teacher Assistant.* Dubuque, Iowa: W. C. Brown, 1972.

James, Margaret T. *School Volunteers.* New York: Public Education Association, 1961.

Johnson, William H. "Utilizing Teacher Aides," *The Clearing House*, *42*:229-233, December, 1967.

Lewis, James. *Differentiating the Teaching Staff.* West Nyack, N.Y.: Parker Publishing Company, 1971.

National Education Association. *Teacher Aides in Public Schools,"* *NEA Research Bulletin*, *45*:37-39, May, 1967.

National School Public Relations Association. *Paraprofessionals in Schools.* Washington, D.C.: The Association, 1972.

Noar, Gertrude. *Teacher Aides at Work.* National Commission on Teacher

Education and Professional Standards. Washington, D.C.: National Education Association, 1967.

York, Lilla J. *The Roles of the Professional and Paraprofessional Personnel in Team Teaching.* Dallas: Leslie, 1971.

Wright, Elizabeth A. *Teacher Aides to the Rescue: Program Guidelines for Better Home-School-Community Partnerships.* New York: John Day, 1969.

INDEX

A

Achievement test results, 40
Aides, (*See* Teacher aides)
Activities, classroom, 114-115
Anecdotal records, 153-154
Assessment of aide's performance, 140-157
Assets, instructional, 40
Assignments, delegating, 25-27
Assignments, teacher aide, 14-15, 63
Attitudes, 142
Audiovisual aids, (*See* Media)

B

Basal reading approach, 80-81
Benefits of teacher aides, 41
Building tour, 10
Bulletin boards, 106-107

C

Cafeteria, 116-118
Certification, teacher aide, 7
Checklist, evaluation, 143-147
Children's literature, 94
Choral reading, 86
Classroom management, 34-36
Classroom materials, 102-103
Classroom observation, 11, 33
Classroom preparation, 45
Classroom regulations, 35
Classroom visitation, 133
Clerical assistants, 41
"Code of Ethics of the Teaching Profession," 15
Communications, 20-21
Community relations, 42-43, 126-127, 139
Community resources, 138-139
Conferences, teacher aide, 22-25, 154-155
Confidential information, 13

Corridor duties, 120-122
Counselor, 122-123
Courtesy, 35
Crandall, Nelson D., 5
Criticism, constructive, 31-32
Curriculum, 59, 61
Curriculum guides, 12

D

Daily activities, 43
Daily planning schedules, 46-48
Daily school program, 60, 62
Decision-making, 17
Delegating assignments, 25-27
Displays, 106-107
Discipline, 14, 36-38, 113-114, 117-118, 120-122
Dolch Basic Word List, 84
Dramatic play, 116
Duties, teacher aide, 3, 4, 8, 12, 43-46, 50-51, 53-54, 59-62, 76, 91, 102, 108

E

Employment process, 7
Ethics, code of, 15
Evaluation, teacher aide performance, 16-18, 140-157
  anecdotal records, 153-154
  checklist, 143-147
  criteria, selecting, 141-143
  elements of a successful program, 141
  instruments, 143-147
  inventory, 143-144
  postevaluation conference, 154-155
  rating scale, 144-145
  self-evaluation, 18, 142, 147-152
Expectations for aides, 20-22, 27
Experiences in the classroom, 10
Extracurricular activities, 124

161